CASKET EMPTY
BIBLE STUDY

New Testament

DAVID L. PALMER & JOHN R. MOSER

Casket Empty Media LLC.

www.casketempty.com

ISBN: 979-8-9867285-0-6

Contents

Introduction

THE NEW TESTAMENT CONSISTS OF twenty-seven books, written by diverse authors, across three generations, yet it completes God's one redemptive story that began in the Old Testament. In this Bible study you will encounter the most important figure in the New Testament, Jesus Christ, the Son of God, our Savior, who is Lord of all. His life, death, and resurrection are central to the storyline of the entire Bible. You will discover other significant people, such as Jesus' disciples, Peter, James, and John, as well as early missionaries like Paul, Luke, Aquila, and Priscilla. You will learn about key events, such as the pouring out of the Holy Spirit at Pentecost, the expanding missionary witness of the church, and the church's faithful perseverance during times of persecution from an unbelieving world.

The premise of the CASKET EMPTY Bible series is that there is a single story of the Bible that makes sense of the individual stories and books. Once you understand this story, individual verses and biblical books fit within the larger narrative. This is particularly important for understanding the New Testament. You may not be aware that one out of every ten verses in the New Testament is an explicit quotation or clear allusion to the Old Testament. The gospel writers connect the coming of Jesus with

God's promises in the Old Testament. Key New Testament topics, such as the kingdom of God, justification by faith, and forgiveness of sins are deeply rooted in the Old Testament. Jesus' own preaching heralds the good news that the time is fulfilled, and the kingdom of God is at hand. He calls people to repent and believe in the gospel. Early Christians understood that all the prophets in the Old Testament bear witness to Jesus. Everyone who believes in him receives forgiveness of sins. The shape of Christian theology is the hope of the Old Testament fulfilled in Christ. There is a breathtaking and coherent vision from Genesis to Revelation. If you are willing to embark on this study of the New Testament over the next fourteen weeks, you will learn about the richness of God's word and how it shapes and informs our lives today.

Since God is the main character of the biblical story, studying the New Testament will reveal God's identity and character, and the wonder of his redemptive plan. Jesus tells his disciples that whoever has seen him has seen the Father. The New Testament shows us that the death and resurrection of Jesus are the focus of God's saving purpose. Jesus is the Lamb of God, who takes away the sin of the world. He is the beloved Son sent forth from the Father's love. He defeats the power of sin and death so that there is no condemnation for those who are in Christ Jesus. His resurrection marks the dawn of God's new creation and the fulfillment of God's promises of old. His bodily resurrection is the firstfruits of those who have died and the guarantee of our own resurrection.

The New Testament points us to the death and resurrection of Jesus as the model for Christian discipleship. Jesus says: "If anyone would come after me, let him deny himself and take up his cross and follow me" (Matt 16:24). We die to self in our daily lives so that we might walk in newness of life. The goal of this study is that you would not only learn the storyline of the New Testament and understand that God's plan of redemption is wonderfully fulfilled in Jesus, but also that you might encounter afresh the living God and be stirred by his steadfast love *for you*. When you experience the love of God in Christ, his love will compel your dedicated service. When you stand in awe of God's saving purpose, you will offer your life to him in grateful response. When your heart rejoices in Christ alone, you will share him with others so that they too may openly worship Jesus the Lamb who was slain. He has ransomed people for God from every tribe, language, people, and nation.

The Story of the Bible Through CASKET EMPTY®

The CASKET EMPTY® curriculum is designed to help you learn the redemptive story of the Bible in a way that is accessible and memorable. In the first week of the study you will be introduced to the acronym CASKET EMPTY, which will help you put the Bible together chronologically and theologically. The story of redemption traced through CASKET EMPTY focuses on six key periods in the Old Testament (CASKET) and five key periods in the New Testament (EMPTY). In our study, you will discover that there is a coherence and unity to the Bible because there is one author, God himself, who inspires human authors, empowered by his Spirit, to write about his saving plan for his creation. This is the true story of the world, the one that gives meaning and purpose to our lives. The Bible is God's living word that speaks directly to us, as we humbly seek his face and listen for his voice.

What to Pack for the Journey

A Bible – Use a version that is easy to read. The ESV, NASB, or NIV are all trusted versions, and study Bibles can be helpful if you want to explore a particular passage or book in more depth. Several Bible apps are available online (such as the popular YouVersion). These apps can be useful, but the advantage of having your own hard copy of the Bible is that you can underline verses that stand out to you and that are key to your study—and you can write in the margins! Reading Bible passages in different versions, such as the NLT or *The Message,* can be helpful at times, giving you more "aha!" moments as you hear God's word afresh in a different translation.

A Study Schedule – If you are doing this Bible study as part of a small group or weekly Bible class, your goal each week is to arrive at your group having read the Bible passages and written your responses to the questions. You can choose to do a smaller portion of the study each day (perhaps 20 minutes), reading and answering several questions each time, or you may want to schedule a block of time once a week. It is helpful to put your reading schedule into your personal calendar so that you develop a regular study pattern.

Bible Study Questions – Each week you will be asked to read four to five chapters from the New Testament, along with selected verses from the Old Testament. Questions on these readings are designed for you to reflect upon a passage and dig deeper. Write out your responses and be prepared to share them with your group. Sometimes you will be asked to fill in a simple chart based on the reading; this is designed to help you organize the content of the passage. If you are unable to answer a particular question, let your leader know so that someone in your group can help you. An openness to asking questions will only enhance your study of God's word and build trust with others in your group. Each week you will be asked to apply what you have studied. While information is important, transformation requires that you reflect more deeply and consider what the Holy Spirit might be saying to you personally. Be prayerful and open yourself up to the transforming power of Jesus.

New Testament Timeline, Maps, and Study Guide

At the end of each weekly study, you will be asked to review the *CASKET EMPTY New Testament Timeline*, along with the relevant map from the *CASKET EMPTY New Testament Maps* (available at casketempty.com). Don't skip over this step. Reviewing the timeline each week will reinforce visually where you are in the biblical story. You should start to notice common themes and patterns that will help you understand how the Old and New Testaments relate to each other theologically. Pictures appearing on the timeline represent important events that have theological significance, and the theological key on the back of the timeline explains each picture. Review of the relevant map will help you identify the geographical location of key events and stories. Over the course of the next fourteen weeks, you will gain a deeper understanding of the geographical movement of Jesus and the early church, as the gospel is being proclaimed among the nations, and as the Scriptures are taught to make disciples in newly formed churches. Readings are also given each week from the *CASKET EMPTY New Testament Study Guide*. While these additional readings are not required, they are highly recommended for those who want to gain a deeper understanding of the New Testament. Chapters in the *Study Guide* are organized according to the acronym EMPTY. This means that if there is a particular period that is less familiar to you, reading the relevant chapter will fill in the gaps and enrich your study of God's word.

Travel Companions

While you can experience this Bible study solo, it will be far richer if you are able to do this study with others. You may want to join your church's Bible class or small group. If a study is not being offered at your church, you could invite someone to do this study with you. If your group is unable to meet in person, this study can be adapted to an online format, which is another way you can walk this journey with others in the Christian community. If at all possible, it is ideal for one person to be the designated leader, as this person can guide you through the questions, encourage you to share your discoveries, and probe further as you grapple with how to apply the passage. Leaders can prepare ahead of time by reading through the *Study Guide*, by referencing the Leader's Guide at the back of this volume, and by watching the videos that are available on the website (casketempty.com).

Companion Old Testament Bible Study

The CASKET EMPTY Bible Study is a two-part series. Eighteen weeks are devoted to the Old Testament (CASKET), and fourteen weeks are devoted to the New Testament (EMPTY). This allows the option of two separate, stand-alone studies, but ideally, they are best done together. This way you can learn the redemptive story of the entire Bible from Genesis to Revelation. As with the New Testament, the *Old Testament Bible Study* is designed to be used with the *Old Testament Timeline, Maps, and Study Guide.*

The Priority of Teaching and Preaching God's Word

With an increasing biblical illiteracy among Christians today, our prayer is that the CASKET EMPTY series will provide resources for the local church. The Scriptures exhort us to devote ourselves to the preaching and teaching of God's word. With so many competing voices that cry out for our attention, it is time to pause and to reflect on what is important. Each generation needs a renewed vision of the centrality of the Scriptures in the life of the church. Our prayer is that this Bible study might rekindle in you a desire to dig deeper into the Scriptures and to discover afresh God's kingdom purpose for your life. With this in mind, the series is ideal for a church-wide curriculum that traces God's plan of redemption through the entire Bible. When done together, both studies provide thirty-two weekly studies that can be done as a yearlong study (allowing for breaks during Advent, Easter, and summer). A concurrent preaching series enables the whole congregation to journey through the story of the Bible together. Pastors are encouraged to follow the outline given in the studies when selecting biblical passages for preaching. The Old and New Testament *Study Guides* provide additional information, and the CASKET EMPTY PowerPoints are a helpful resource for teaching in larger groups. Short videos are also available online, providing further background and teaching tips (casketempty.com).

May the LORD bless the preaching and teaching of his word!
David Palmer and John Moser

One Redemptive Story

THE NEW TESTAMENT COMPLETES GOD'S one redemptive story from Matthew to Revelation. In Jesus Christ, God sends his beloved Son into the world to fulfill his saving purpose for the world. Jesus begins his public preaching with the breathtaking announcement that the time is fulfilled, and the kingdom of God is at hand. The hope of the Old Testament prophets has arrived at last. Jesus calls his hearers to repent and believe the gospel. This marks the beginning of new life by faith. Jesus summons men, women, and children to follow him. They become his disciples and learn to walk in his ways. Jesus demonstrates the reality of God's kingdom and reveals himself to be the promised King, the long-awaited Messiah. He is the solution to sin, death, and evil. As Messiah, Jesus carries the sin of the world to the cross. His suffering and death provide atonement, the forgiveness of sins. Three days later, his tomb is empty, and he is found alive! Jesus' resurrection testifies that death has been defeated and God's new creation has begun. There is one redemptive story of the Bible, and Jesus is at its center. He is the climax of the story. This is why his death and resurrection are represented in the title for the CASKET EMPTY series.

Jesus calls his followers to share this good news with all the world. He promises that he will never leave us nor forsake us. He will give the Holy Spirit to empower our faithful witness among all people and nations. Jesus sends his followers to proclaim the good news of the kingdom across cultural, geographical, and societal boundaries. God's one redemptive story is good news for all the earth. Many will come from the east and west to feast at the banquet table in the kingdom of God, alongside people like Abraham, Isaac, and Jacob. No one is denied an invitation to the marriage supper of the Lamb. Expanding witness to Jesus' death and resurrection radiates out to Africa, Asia, Europe, and beyond. New Testament letters encourage disciples and strengthen the church to grow in faith. Jesus himself builds the church, the gathered assembly of all who believe in him. The power of hell cannot prevail. No human scheme can prevent his purpose. He will gather a people for himself. They will be for the praise of his glory. They are a community of forgiven sinners, reconciled to one another and committed to justice in the land. They call all people to repent and believe, finding forgiveness in his name. All who receive Jesus Christ are adopted into his family and bear his honorable name as Christians. Their eyes are fixed upon their Savior who died and rose again. Their lives are increasingly patterned after him. They share Christ without fear and do not waver under persecution or threat. They walk away from temptation that would disgrace or discredit his holy name. They reject teaching that would direct them away from the sound of his voice. They are his body, his bride. They are his beloved who serve him boldly on the earth and eagerly await his glorious return. God's one redemptive story fills their hearts with his love and overflows in their love for him.

Arrangement of the Books of the New Testament

As we follow God's plan of redemption in the New Testament, it is important that you are able to locate individual books within the storyline. The New Testament is comprised of twenty-seven books, yet in order to read them in their correct time period and historical setting, we need to place each book in its original context. The individual books in the New Testament are organized according to genre. There are four different types of material in the New Testament: gospels, history, letters, and prophecy. The first four books of the New Testament are called gospels, since they focus on the good news that Jesus, the promised Messiah, has come. The four gospels are Matthew, Mark, Luke, and John. The second type of material is history (Acts). This does not mean that other New Testament books are not historical records, but rather, the book of Acts is identified as history since Luke records the historical events that take place after Jesus' ascension to the Father. The third type of material consists of letters. There are twenty-one letters. The letters are written to early church communities to provide instruction on Christian doctrine and identity, and how the people of God are to live as followers of Jesus. As you read through the New Testament letters, it is important to realize they are not arranged in chronological order. Instead, the twenty-one letters are grouped together by author: thirteen letters of Paul (Romans-Philemon), one letter by the writer of Hebrews, one letter by James, two letters by Peter (1-2 Peter), three letters by John (1-3 John), and one letter by Jude. For each author, the letters are arranged by descending length. For example, Romans is the first of Paul's letters in the New Testament because it is the longest and Philemon is Paul's final letter because it is the shortest. The fourth type of material is prophecy. There is one book of prophecy, Revelation. This book reveals to us an extended vision of Jesus' present rule and future glory at his return. The acronym

EMPTY will help you trace the storyline of the New Testament and locate individual books within each period.

Learning the Acronym CASKET EMPTY

The story of the Bible is traced through six periods in the Old Testament (CASKET), and five periods in the New Testament (EMPTY). Each period has its own heading and date:

C = Creation (date uncertain)
A = Abraham (2100–1450 BC)
S = Sinai (1450–1050 BC)
K = Kings (1050–586 BC)
E = Exile (586–539 BC)
T = Temple (539–430 BC)

E = Expectations (430–6 BC)
M = Messiah (6 BC–AD 33)
P = Pentecost (AD 33–65)
T = Teaching (AD 33–95)
Y = Yet-to-come (AD 95–Return of Christ)

Each heading is a summary of the particular period, and the first letter of each heading makes up the acronym CASKET EMPTY. It will greatly benefit your study of the New Testament if you are able to memorize the headings and the dates of each period in the acronym EMPTY as early as possible. This will help you locate biblical books within their correct time period. Committing to memory the five pictures on the timeline that represent the five periods of the New Testament will enable you to rehearse the main plot of the story. When read together with the Old Testament, the title CASKET EMPTY points to Jesus' empty tomb as the fulfillment of God's redemptive plan. This is the story of the Bible—with Jesus at the center.

Conversation Starters

To get the conversation started, share with your class or study group your impression of the New Testament. Check as many as apply!

I think that the New Testament:
- ❑ Realistically portrays the disciples of Jesus
- ❑ Includes miracles which I find hard to accept
- ❑ Repeats itself too much – why are there four different gospels?
- ❑ Is all about loving Jesus and his mission
- ❑ Presents a "loving God" in contrast to the Old Testament's "angry God"
- ❑ Makes me feel like I am right there as an eyewitness to the actions
- ❑ other: _____

My favorite New Testament book is _____, because…

The thing I find most difficult to understand about the New Testament is…

In this Bible study I hope to...
- ❑ learn more about the New Testament
- ❑ have some of my questions about the Bible answered
- ❑ grow closer with others in my church
- ❑ grow in my relationship with God
- ❑ know more about what it means to be a Christian since I'm new to the faith
- ❑ other: _____

Bible Readings:
Luke 24:27, 44-49; Romans 1:1-4; 1 Corinthians 15:3-4

Questions for Reflection

1. Read Luke 24:27, 44-49. What do Jesus' words teach us about how we are to approach the Old Testament (called the "Scriptures")? What portions of the Old Testament Scriptures are written about Jesus?

2. How does Jesus' teaching to his disciples demonstrate that the Bible is one redemptive story? How does Jesus' view of the Scriptures shape how we are to read the Bible?

3. Read Romans 1:1-4. Does it surprise you to read that God promised the *gospel* beforehand in the Old Testament Scriptures? Notice also that Jesus is God's Son "descended from David according to the flesh." This recalls the promise made to King David in the Old Testament that his descendent would be God's Son (2 Sam. 7:14; cf. Ps. 2:7). The Bible truly is *the story of God's redemptive plan with Jesus at the center.* What stands out to you or surprises you in these verses?

4. Read 1 Corinthians 15:3-4. How does Paul understand the Old Testament Scriptures in relation to Jesus? What aspects of the Scriptures does he highlight that point to Jesus?

5. What does Paul say is of "first importance"? How is Paul's teaching in this verse represented in the CASKET EMPTY acronym? What would you say is of "first importance" in your life?

6. As we begin our study of the New Testament, it is helpful for you to review the acronym EMPTY, along with the pictures. Use this chart as a guide to help you learn the five key periods in the New Testament. Be prepared to share your summaries with others in your group.

What does each letter represent?	What is the picture for each period?	Give a 2-3 sentence summary for each period
E =		
M =		
P =		

T =		
Y =		

Dig Deeper with the *Study Guide*
❑ Read the introduction (pp. *xi-xix*)

Expectations for a Coming King

WE BEGIN OUR STUDY OF the New Testament by becoming familiar with what takes place in the intertestamental period. The term "intertestamental" may be new to you, but it refers to the four hundred years in between the Old and New Testaments, covering the period after Malachi but before Matthew. Many people wrongly imagine this as a period of divine silence or inactivity. To be sure, there is no inspired prophetic voice adding to the canon of Scripture during this time. However, just as God used the four hundred years of slavery in Egypt to prepare his people for redemption through the Exodus, God will use these four hundred years to prepare the world for redemption through his Son. Throughout this period, God builds expectations for a coming king both in Israel and among the nations. There are two important and related movements in this intertestamental period, as God's people wait for the promises given by God to be fulfilled. First, the nations of the world are brought into greater contact with God's people and are given access to the sacred Scriptures. The nations are attracted to the living God, who is holy and righteous in all his ways. Second, God's people are humbled through suffering and refined through trial. They search the Old Testament Scriptures and eagerly await the fulfillment of his promises.

The LORD God sovereignly directs history during these four hundred years according to his word given to the prophet Daniel. If you have studied the Old Testament, you may remember that the Babylonian king Nebuchadnezzar dreams of a statue with a head of gold, chest of silver, thighs of bronze and feet mixed with iron and clay. Then, a stone cut without human hands strikes the statue, smashing it to pieces that are blown away by the wind. The stone, however, rises like a great mountain and fills the earth. At that time (over five hundred years before Jesus), God gives Daniel the interpretation of this vision as a sequence of four earthly kingdoms: Babylon, Persia, Greece, and Rome. The stone represents a fifth kingdom, *the kingdom of God*, which will supplant all others and endure forever. Daniel himself later dreams of a storm-tossed sea out of which four terrifying beasts arise. These creatures exercise dominion with violence and terrorize those under their rule. Suddenly the heavens open to reveal God seated on a glorious and exalted throne. The dominion of the beasts is taken away as a fifth figure, a Son of Man, receives an everlasting kingdom that will never be destroyed. He will reign forever in righteousness. All peoples, nations, and languages will one day worship him. He will bring God's salvation to the world.

As the intertestamental period draws to a close, God's people know that the next movement of history will be the arrival of God's kingdom. The promises of the Old Testament prophets will come true. The kingdom of God will extend over all the earth. The royal Son of Man will rule forever. The Son of David will be restored to his throne. Atonement for the sin of the world will be made. A new covenant will be inscribed upon the human heart. The Holy Spirit will be poured out upon all humanity. The blessing of Abraham will extend to all nations. There will be a resurrection from the dead. There will be a final judgment and evil will be condemned. God will create a new heaven and a new earth in which righteousness dwells. The hope of Israel rises in our hearts as we look forward for our God to act. He will do so in Jesus Christ. These are the expectations that prepare us for the arrival of Jesus, the long-awaited Messiah.

Bible Readings:
Isaiah 11:1-10; Daniel 2:1-45; 7:1-28; Mark 14:61-62

Questions for Reflection

1. Read Daniel 2:1-18. The book of Daniel was read and studied during the intertestamental period, along with other Old Testament Scriptures. Summarize in your own words what Nebuchadnezzar sees in his dream.

2. Read Daniel 2:19-43. How does Daniel interpret the four kingdoms in Nebuchadnezzar's dream? Which kingdoms belong to Daniel's own lifetime and which kingdoms belong to the intertestamental period?

First kingdom (Babylonian):

Second kingdom (Persian):

Third kingdom (Greek):

Fourth kingdom (Roman):

3. Read Daniel 2:34-35, 44-45. How does Daniel interpret the fifth kingdom? How does the "stone" smash the pretentious kingdoms of our world and what does it become?

4. How might Daniel 2 build expectations about the kingdom of God during the intertestamental period? What might God's people be expecting?

5. If you heard Jesus announce that the "kingdom of God was at hand," what would you be expecting him to do in light of Daniel's prophecy?

6. Read Daniel 7:1-8. How does Daniel describe the four kingdoms he saw in his dream? How does his vision compare with Nebuchadnezzar's dream?

First kingdom (Babylonian):

Second kingdom (Persian):

Third kingdom (Greek):

Fourth kingdom (Roman):

7. Read Daniel 7:9-14. Describe what Daniel sees. How is his vision of the fifth kingdom different from the preceding four kingdoms? What stands out to you?

8. Read Mark 14:61-62. When Jesus is asked if he is the Messiah, Jesus responds by quoting Daniel 7:13. How does his use of Daniel's prophecy point to himself? What does this tell you about Jesus' identity?

9. Read Isaiah 11:1-10. As you reflect on this passage, remember that some trees, when cut down to a stump, will eventually produce a shoot or branch that grows to produce fruit, but only after many, long years. How does Isaiah's use of this imagery provide a helpful picture of the period of EXPECTATIONS when God's people have to wait a long time for the promised king from the line of Jesse? What will the Messiah, the shoot of Jesse be like? How will the world begin to change when he arrives?

Applying God's Word

1. How was God actively working in history during the period of EXPECTATIONS? What might this teach us about the way God works in our own lives, even when we don't fully understand what he is doing?

2. Put yourself in Israel's place during the period of EXPECTATIONS. How might you have felt when it seemed as though the nations of the world were prospering? How might having a vision of the coming kingdom of God give you hope?

3. Jesus often refers to himself as the "Son of Man," yet he also teaches his disciples that the Son of Man did not come "to be served but to serve, and give his life as a ransom for many" (Mark 10:45). Reflect upon this verse in light of the exalted and glorious Son of Man in Daniel 7. What do you notice?

4. Ask the Holy Spirit to open your eyes to behold Jesus in his full glory as the exalted Son of Man who rules over God's everlasting kingdom, and also as God's devoted servant, who gives his life as a ransom for you. Write out a prayer of thanksgiving to God.

Review Timeline and Map

❑ Review the EXPECTATIONS section on the New Testament timeline and familiarize yourself with the specific Old Testament promises upon which Israel based their expectations of the Messiah.

❑ Review the first New Testament map, *The World of Expectations*. Note the boundaries of the Greek and Roman Empires.

Dig Deeper with the *Study Guide*

❑ Read chapter one: EXPECTATIONS (pp. 1-55).

Jesus Our Messiah Has Come

WHEN WE OPEN THE NEW Testament, we breathe an atmosphere of fulfillment. God's redemptive purpose is coming to fruition in Jesus Christ. The four hundred years of waiting are finally over. All four gospels share the life-giving belief that Jesus our Savior has come. The four gospel writers, Matthew, Mark, Luke, and John, interpret the arrival of Jesus as the hope of Israel and present his ministry as the hope of the entire world.

Matthew opens with a moving statement that his book is about "Jesus Christ, the son of David, the son of Abraham" (Matt. 1:1). Jesus is Israel's Messiah, David's promised son. He is Abraham's descendant who brings blessing to all nations. Matthew's genealogy moves forward from Abraham to David, then from David to the exile, and finally, from the exile to the Messiah. These three movements mark key turning points in God's sovereign plan of redemption that find their fulfillment in Jesus. Matthew teaches that the birth of Jesus signals the end of the exile. God's glorious presence has returned in Jesus, who is Immanuel, "God with us." Matthew records the arrival of wise men from the east, who follow the star of Bethlehem to worship the newborn King. Israel's prophets foresaw that one day, all nations would come to the light of God's glory and learn to walk in his ways.

Mark introduces his gospel this way: "The beginning of the gospel of Jesus Christ, the Son of God" (Mark 1:1). Jesus is the Messiah, the Son of God. In him, the hope of Israel is fulfilled. Jesus is the divine Son of God to whom kingship, authority, and power rightly belong. Mark locates the beginning of the gospel with the ministry of John the Baptist, the messianic herald in the wilderness. God had promised through Malachi, the last prophet in the Old Testament: "Behold, I send my messenger, and he will prepare the way before me" (Mal. 3:1). God had announced a highway of redemption where "the glory of the LORD shall be revealed, and all flesh shall see it together" (Isa. 40:5). In Jesus Christ, the Son of God, the promised second Exodus has arrived. All humanity will see it together.

Luke focuses on "the things that have been accomplished among us" (Luke 1:1). His gospel begins as the Lord gives a son to an elderly and barren couple named Zechariah and Elizabeth. Their son will be John the Baptist. The angel Gabriel announces to Mary the birth of the Messiah himself. She blesses the God of Israel "for he has visited and redeemed his people and has raised up a horn of salvation for us in the house of his servant David, as he spoke by the mouth of his holy prophets from of old" (Luke 1:68-70). The birth of Jesus brings hope for the world. Angels announce to shepherds in Bethlehem good news of great joy for all people. When Joseph and Mary dedicate Jesus in the temple courts, an elderly man named Simeon blesses God for his salvation and declares that Jesus is "a light for revelation to the Gentiles, and glory to your people Israel" (Luke 2:32). The coming of Jesus our Savior is good news for all.

John begins his gospel with a poetic prologue that evokes the creation in Genesis: "In the beginning was the Word, and the

Word was with God, and the Word was God" (John 1:1). Jesus is the Word, the divine Son of God, equal with the Father. He is uncreated, eternal, and full of light. John's prologue reaches a climax with the declaration that "the Word became flesh and dwelt among us, and we have seen his glory, glory as of the only Son from the Father, full of grace and truth" (John 1:14). Jesus tabernacles among us as the incarnate Son of God. He makes visible the invisible God. All who receive him become children of God. All four of the gospel writers share the belief that Jesus is the promised Messiah, the Son of God. He fulfills the hope of Israel and brings salvation to the world. "For God so loved the world, that he gave his only Son, that whoever believes in him should not perish but have eternal life" (John 3:16).

Bible Readings:
2 Samuel 7:12-16; Isaiah 40:1-5; Matthew 1:1–2:12; Mark 1:1-15; Luke 1:1-38 and John 1:1-18

Questions for Reflection

1. Read Matthew 1:1. Jesus is identified in the opening verse as the Messiah (Christ), the son of David, the son of Abraham. How does this *one* verse encapsulate the story of redemption in the Old Testament?

2. Read Matthew 1:1-25. This passage records the genealogy of Jesus in three segments of fourteen generations. Why do you think Matthew rooted Jesus' story so strongly in this "Old Testament History Lesson"? What does this tell you about who Jesus is?

3. In theatrical work, the "stand in" is placed on stage to test the lighting, sound, and spacing with other actors before the "star" comes on the stage in front of the live audience. How have all the Israelite kings in Matthew's genealogy acted as "stand ins" (though sometimes not very godly) before the coming of Jesus, the Messiah? What makes Jesus different from *every* other king?

4. Read Matthew 2:1-12. Why was Jesus' birth in Bethlehem so important? Do you remember what famous king was also from Bethlehem (see 1 Sam. 16)? How do the magi respond to Jesus and what does this tell you about his identity?

5. Read Mark 1:1-15. How is John the Baptist the fulfillment of the prophecy in Isaiah 40:1-5? How does John prepare people for Jesus? Who is Jesus in light of Isaiah's prophetic expectation?

6. Read Luke 1:1-38. How does Luke's introduction in 1:1-4 underline the veracity and historicity of the life of Jesus? What questions have you wrestled with regarding the trustworthiness of the gospel accounts?

7. God promised King David that his descendant would rule on God's throne over his everlasting kingdom (see 2 Sam. 7:12-16). How is Jesus identified in Luke's gospel in 1:26-38? What does this tell you about his identity and mission?

8. Read John 1:1-18. What do these opening verses tell you about Jesus' relationship to God the Father? How does Jesus make the Father known to us?

Applying God's Word

1. Eugene Peterson (author of *The Message* translation of the Bible) calls the four gospel writers "The Gospel Quartet," making the point that all four are singing the same song about Jesus, but each sings a different "part" that harmonizes with the others. Would you agree with Peterson? Based on what we have studied so far, give a one-to-three-word headline for each gospel writer's work. Which description of Jesus resonates with you and why?

2. When the magi encounter Jesus, they bow down and worship him. How would you characterize your relationship with Jesus? Has there been a time in your life when you have, literally, bowed down in worship, recognizing that Jesus is God's exalted king who rules over the kingdom of God?

3. The gospel writers all begin by showing that the Old Testament hope finds its fulfillment in Jesus. How does this conviction produce hope in you today? Who do you know who needs this message of hope?

4. What areas of your own life need to come under the Lordship of Jesus?

Review Timeline and Map
- ❑ Review the MESSIAH section on the timeline.
- ❑ Review the second New Testament map, *Israel in the Time of Jesus.*

Dig Deeper with the *Study Guide*
- ❑ Read chapter two: MESSIAH, PART 1 (pp. 57-93).

Jesus Proclaims the Kingdom

JESUS BEGINS HIS PUBLIC MINISTRY with the stirring announcement that "the time is fulfilled, and the kingdom of God is at hand" (Mark 1:15). The announcement of the kingdom indicates the arrival of the long-awaited righteous reign of God upon the earth. The original calling of humanity was to reflect God's image and his wise rule over his creation, but human beings fell short of God's original design. Lives characterized by idolatry deface the image of God and damage both people and God's good creation. Jesus' announcement of the kingdom calls people to "repent and believe." Jesus calls twelve disciples to come follow him. The invitation is given to all of us to turn away from sin and place our trust in Jesus as Savior. Jesus calls us to follow him and commit ourselves to learn his ways, as a community of his disciples.

The central theme of Jesus' teaching is the arrival of the kingdom of God. In his Sermon on the Mount, Jesus confers the blessing of the kingdom on all who follow him. He explains that life in the kingdom is one of consecrated obedience to the revealed will of God. He expounds the meaning of the sacred Scriptures and teaches his followers about who they are and how they are to live as citizens of God's kingdom. They are the salt of the earth. They are the light of the world. They are to seek his kingdom first. They reject the methods, models, and measures of worldly success. They take Jesus seriously. They pursue the virtues of his kingdom by serving others and by practicing self-denial so that others might glorify the Father. Jesus' sermon ends with three powerful images: a narrow and wide gate, a fruitful and unfruitful tree, a wise and foolish builder. Only those who hear the words of Jesus and put them into practice will flourish.

Jesus demonstrates the arrival of the kingdom by healing the sick, casting out demons, and by performing prophetic signs. He comes to bring forgiveness for sinners, restoration for the broken, and recovery for the lost. His healings indicate that he has come for those who are sick and suffering. Jesus will carry our diseases. His casting out of demons means that he has come to free those afflicted by demonic oppression and the false promises of sin. Jesus will conquer the devil and free his captives. Jesus' prophetic signs reveal that the time of fulfillment is at hand. He is the prophet who was to come into the world. He is the bread of life who will be broken for our salvation. He is the good shepherd who will lay his life down for us. He is the way, the truth, and the life. All who believe in him will receive eternal life.

Jesus proclaims the arrival of the kingdom of God in parables. Parables are a prophetic way of speaking that is rooted in the Old Testament. A parable invites the hearer inside the story and requires a response of faith. Jesus' parables reveal his identity and announce the arrival of his kingdom. At the end of every parable, we should always ask two questions: "Who is Jesus Christ revealed to be in this parable?" and "What does he require of us in response?"

A decisive turning point in the gospels takes place when Jesus asks his disciples: "Who do you say that I am?" (Matt. 16:15). Peter steps forward and solemnly confesses: "You are the Christ, the Son of the living God" (Matt. 16:16). Each of us must answer Jesus' question for ourselves. If you have never prayed to receive Christ, I urge you to do so right now. After Peter's great confession of faith, Jesus explains the meaning of his messiahship. He begins to show his disciples that as Messiah "he must go to Jerusalem and suffer many things from the elders and chief priests and scribes, and be killed, and on the third day be raised" (Matt. 16:21). The Son of Man comes not to be served but to serve and give his life as a ransom for us. It is in this ancient city of Jerusalem that God's redemptive story for all the world will be accomplished.

Bible Readings:
Deuteronomy 18:15-18; Matthew 5–7; 16:13-23; Mark 1:14-20; 3:13-19; Luke 15 and John 6

Questions for Reflection

1. Read Mark 1:14-20. Jesus begins his public ministry with the announcement of the kingdom of God. What does this tell you about Jesus' identity and God's promises in the Old Testament? What are the "entry requirements" for the kingdom?

2. How would each of these groups react to hearing Jesus declare, "The kingdom of God is at hand!"?

The poor and oppressed

Roman military and political leaders

Jewish religious and political leaders

What does this announcement mean to *you?*

3. Read Mark 1:16-20 and Mark 3:13-19. Peter, Andrew, James, and John were fishing. Matthew (Levi) was working in his tax collection booth. Others encounter Jesus. A Samaritan woman was drawing water from a well. Martha was serving food at a dinner party. As we read the gospels, we can place ourselves right there at the lakeshore, in the tax booth, at the well, and at the dinner party. What were you doing when Jesus called *you?*

4. Read Matthew 5:1-12: The Sermon on the Mount is Jesus' vivid description of how people experience life in the kingdom of God. Which of these "blessings" (also known as "beatitudes") comfort you? Which ones baffle you? Which ones give you strength and resolve?

5. Read Matthew 5:13–7:29. Jesus declares that he has not come to abolish the law but to fulfill it. In his sermon, Jesus expounds upon the law to show *how* God's people are to live out the ethics of the kingdom. How does Jesus paint a picture of what it means for his followers to exhibit "kingdom living" with regards to anger, sexual temptation, marriage, keeping our promises, revenge, and how to treat your enemy?

6. Read Matthew 16:13-23. What does Peter understand about Jesus and how does he know this? What does Peter clearly NOT yet understand about Jesus?

7. Read Luke 15. Jesus begins teaching about the kingdom in parables in Luke 14:7-35. He tells three more parables in Luke 15. Who is Jesus in these parables? Who are the "lost" and what part does repentance play in the third parable? How does Jesus want *you* to respond?

8. Read John 6. After Jesus feeds the people, what is the reaction of the crowds in John 6:14? Recall God's promise in Deuteronomy 18:15, 18. What does God require of us according to Jesus in John 6:29? After many people turned back from following Jesus near the end of this chapter, what compelled Peter and the others to remain?

Applying God's Word

1. Read Matthew 16:15-16. If Jesus were to ask you this question what would *your* answer be? How have you come to know this?

2. Read Matthew 16:13-20. In this story Peter has an "aha!" moment (revealed to him by God) when he confesses that Jesus is the Messiah. What are the wonderful consequences of Peter's confession of faith in Jesus? As a follower of Jesus, how has God called you to serve him?

Review Timeline and Map

❑ Review the Messiah section on the timeline and note the ways that Jesus fulfills the messianic expectations of Israel.
❑ Review the third New Testament Map: *Jesus' Public Ministry*, noting *where* Jesus demonstrates the kingdom with signs and parables.

Dig Deeper with the Study Guide

❑ Read the first section of chapter 3: MESSIAH, Part 2 (pp. 95-116).

Jesus Is Crucified and Resurrected

THE GOSPEL WRITERS DEVOTE MOST of their attention to Jesus' final week. Holy Week begins with Jesus' dramatic entrance into Jerusalem on Palm Sunday. He intentionally enacts the prophetic imagery of Zechariah, who saw hundreds of years earlier that the Messiah would enter Jerusalem bearing salvation and riding on a donkey. The vast pilgrimage crowds recognize the significance of Jesus' entry into the city and rejoice. They wave palm branches as symbols of victory and shout: "Hosanna to the Son of David! Blessed is he who comes in the name of the Lord! Hosanna in the highest!" (Matt. 21:9). Although some of the religious leaders urge Jesus to rebuke the crowds, he tells them that if these people were silent, the very stones would cry out! As Jesus approaches Jerusalem, he begins to weep over it. This is the moment of God's visitation, but many do not yet understand what is required to make peace.

As Jesus' final hour approaches, he gathers his disciples to celebrate the Passover. As the meal is being served, Jesus astonishes them by washing their feet. The Lord of glory, the incarnate Son of God, takes the form of a servant. He had told them earlier that the Son of Man came not to be served but to serve and to give his life as a ransom for many. Jesus interprets the central symbols of the Passover meal around himself. He takes bread, breaks it, and gives it to his disciples, saying, "This is my body, which is given for you" (Luke 22:19). In this meal Jesus teaches his disciples that *he* is the Passover Lamb offered for them. Jesus takes the cup and declares, "This cup that is poured out for you is the new covenant in my blood" (Luke 22:20). God's promise spoken through the prophet Jeremiah is being fulfilled. The new covenant is being established, and forgiveness is made available in the blood of Jesus, the Lamb of God.

Later that evening, Jesus journeys to the Garden of Gethsemane and begins to pray. His soul is in anguish as he anticipates the redemptive mission before him. He holds in his hands the cup of God's wrath against the sin of the world, and his sweat falls like drops of blood. Judas Iscariot appears with an armed crowd and betrays the Son of Man with a kiss. Jesus is brought before Caiaphas the high priest during the night. He is condemned for blasphemy before the Sanhedrin. They spit in Jesus' face and strike him with their fists. In the morning, Jesus is brought before the Roman governor Pontius Pilate. He is accused of being "King of the Jews" and is seen as a threat to Roman order. Pilate makes an initial attempt to release Jesus, but his resolve crumbles under pressure. Although he rightly declares: "I find no guilt in him" (John 18:38), he then hands Jesus over to be mocked, beaten, and flogged. Roman soldiers twist a crown of thorns on his head, and they mockingly array him in a royal purple robe. They put a reed in his right hand, kneel before him, and mock him, saying, "Hail, King of the Jews!" Pilate condemns Jesus to be crucified. Jesus is led outside the walls of the city, like a lamb being led to the slaughter. He is stripped of his garments and forced to carry the wooden crossbeam for his own execution. He is pierced through the median nerve with large iron nails and is lifted up onto a fixed vertical beam, as a third nail is driven through his feet. Pilate affixes a title to identify his name and crime: "Jesus of Nazareth, the King of the Jews." While hanging upon the cross, he is despised, rejected, and mocked by those he came to save. Darkness fills the sky from noon to 3 PM. Jesus cries out in soulful anguish as God's wrath against sin is fully satisfied. Thirsting at the point of death, Jesus completes his saving mission and declares: "It is finished" (John 19:30). Jesus' body is removed from the cross and placed in a freshly hewn tomb. A massive stone is rolled over the entrance. Soldiers guard and seal the tomb, recalling his words that after three days, he would rise.

Early at the dawn of the first day of the week, women bring spices to anoint the body of Jesus. They encounter a powerful earthquake as an angel of the Lord rolls back the stone from the tomb. The angel announces the good news that Jesus has been resurrected from the dead: "Do not be afraid, for I know that you seek Jesus who was crucified. He is not here, for he has risen, as he said" (Matt. 28:5-6). This marks a climactic moment in the story of the entire Bible—Jesus has risen! He later appears to the gathered disciples and declares *peace*—something that only his death could achieve. Jesus' death and resurrection are the decisive events in God's plan of redemption and the guiding image of our CASKET EMPTY study. The gospel narrative ends as Jesus sends his followers out to make disciples of all nations. He promises the presence of the Holy Spirit to empower their witness to his life, death, and resurrection.

Questions for Reflection

1. Read Zechariah 9:9-10 and then read Matthew 21:1-11. How
    does Jesus' arrival into Jerusalem, as foretold by the prophet
    Zechariah, describe the character of his kingship?

2. Read Mark 10:45. How did Jesus' death pay the "ransom" he
    speaks about here?

3. Read Jeremiah 31:31-34 and then read Luke 22:14-20. What is
    Jesus communicating to his disciples by holding the cup and
    identifying it as the blood of the covenant? How does Jesus'
    death secure *your* forgiveness?

4. Imagine that you are sitting at the table in the Upper Room
    with Jesus and his disciples, listening to his words, touch-
    ing and tasting the bread and wine he blesses, breaks, and
    shares. Describe what you might be feeling, experiencing, or
    wondering.

5. Read Isaiah 53:1-12 and then John 19:1-30. What feelings or
    emotions stir in you as you read these two deeply moving pas-
    sages of Scripture?

6. Read Matthew 28:1-15. Jesus had revealed that he would not only die but be raised up three days later (Matt. 16:21; 17:23). Who are the witnesses to these events and how do they respond to the empty tomb and to Jesus' appearance?

Applying God's Word

1. When you take communion (also called the Lord's Supper or the Eucharist) at your church, what thoughts or emotions stir in you as you reflect upon the Lord's death? Is there something especially meaningful to you about this practice? How might the Bible passages we have studied this week prepare your heart and mind to partake of this sacrament?

2. Read Matthew 28:16-20. What is your role in the Great Commission today, both individually and corporately in your local church?

3. How does the truth of the resurrection empower you to live out the Great Commission? What steps might you take this week to reprioritize and reorient your life toward obeying Christ's call to make disciples and teach them to obey all that he commanded us?

4. How might you dialogue with a friend or neighbor who doubts the historicity of the resurrection? How do the four gospel accounts provide credibility for the resurrection of Jesus? What might you point them to in the text that has given you confidence that Jesus truly rose from the dead?

Review Timeline and Map

❑ Review the Messiah section on the timeline. Note the events that transpire as Jesus moves toward the cross.

❑ Review the fourth New Testament Map: *Jesus' Journey to the Cross*. Note the numbered sequence of events that shows the progression of events during the final week of Jesus' life.

Dig Deeper with the Study Guide

❑ Read the second section of chapter 3: MESSIAH, Part 2 (pp. 116-128).

The Holy Spirit Is Poured Out

AFTER HIS RESURRECTION, JESUS PROMISES his disciples that they will receive power when the Holy Spirit comes upon them. The Holy Spirit is God's personal, empowering presence. The Holy Spirit was present at creation and later filled the tabernacle in the wilderness and the temple in Jerusalem with the glory of God. The prophet Ezekiel had seen a vision of God's Spirit breathing new life into his people, raising them to new life and causing them to walk in God's ways. The Old Testament prophets saw the day coming when the Holy Spirit would be poured out on all humanity. Jesus now tells his followers that the Holy Spirit will empower them to be his witnesses in Jerusalem, in all Judea and Samaria, and to the end of the earth. The Holy Spirit opens our heart to believe and then motivates our dedicated service to Jesus. The Holy Spirit encourages us to share Jesus with our family, friends, and even our enemies. The Holy Spirit emboldens us across cultural and societal divisions to offer the good news of God's grace for all. The Holy Spirit creates an active desire for holiness in our lives and inspires us to live like Christ in society. The Holy Spirit fills each person with spiritual gifts that are used to strengthen the entire church community.

When the day of Pentecost arrives, fifty days after Passover, Jesus pours out the Holy Spirit upon all who are gathered in his name. God's presence dwells among Jesus' disciples, like the pillar of cloud and fire that led Israel out of Egypt, and like the fiery divine presence on Mount Sinai. The Holy Spirit empowers Jesus' disciples to proclaim the mighty works of God in the diverse languages of the nations who have assembled in Jerusalem for the Feast of Pentecost. Peter stands up and preaches to those gathered, interpreting these momentous events in light of Joel's prophetic word given to Israel hundreds of years earlier. The prophet had seen that in the last days, God would pour out his Spirit on all mankind and at that time, everyone who called on the name of the LORD would be saved. Peter proclaims that God has exalted Jesus, who was not only crucified but resurrected from the dead and lives forever. Jesus is the promised Messiah and Lord of all. He now pours out the Holy Spirit upon all who believe, both men and women, young and old. Everyone who calls upon the name of the Lord Jesus will be saved! Three thousand people respond to Peter's message and put their faith in Jesus for salvation. They are publicly baptized and call Jesus their Lord. All who believe in Jesus receive forgiveness of sins, the gift of the Holy Spirit, and a place within the growing community of faith, the church.

The outpouring of the Holy Spirit marks the first act of the exalted Jesus and the beginning of the global mission of the church. The narrative of Acts describes the growth of the church under the Lordship of Jesus. In Luke's first book (the gospel of Luke), he emphasizes all that Jesus *began* to do and teach until he was taken up into heaven. In his second book (Acts), Luke presents all that Jesus *continues* to do in the world through his disciples from his exalted place at the right hand of the Father. The expanding

Christian mission in the world is led by Jesus' strong, wise, and sovereign hand. Christian life, mission, and witness are empowered by the Holy Spirit. Throughout his public ministry, Jesus had proclaimed the arrival of the kingdom of God. Through his atoning death on the cross, Jesus redeems the lives of men, women, and children from every nation, who become part of his kingdom. Jesus now actively pursues them, using his disciples, who are empowered by the Holy Spirit. All who believe in Jesus gather in local church communities filled with God's presence. They are the Body of Christ, the Bride of Christ, the Church, the beginning of God's renewed humanity in the world.

Bible Readings:
Joel 2:28-32; Luke 24:44-53; Acts 1:1-14; 2:1-47

Questions for Reflection

1. Read Luke 24:44-53. What are the central tenets of the gospel message based on the risen Christ's description of himself? What does Jesus tell his disciples will happen after his ascension?

2. Read Acts 1:1-14. With Jesus' ascension to heaven, what might the disciples expect to experience based on Jesus' promise to them in Acts 1:8? How will Jesus continue to be at work in the world? How is his ongoing work mediated?

3. Read Acts 2:1-4. What do you notice about how the Holy Spirit's arrival is described? What are the sounds, feelings, and sights experienced by those gathered in Jerusalem?

4. Read Acts 2:5-13. We see the people's questioning and amazed responses to the events that follow Pentecost. What does the wide variety of ethnicities represented in those who hear the words spoken through the Spirit tell us about God's plan of redemption? How does Pentecost anticipate the multi-ethnic church that is being formed?

5. Read Joel 2:28-32 and then read Acts 2:14-36. Why does Peter quote from the prophet Joel and how does it help us understand the significance of the Spirit in these "last days"? How does Peter weave other Old Testament passages into his sermon and why does he quote them (see Pss. 16:8-11; 110:1)?

6. The prophet Joel prophesied that the pouring out of the Spirit would be accompanied by people calling on the name of the LORD (the name Yahweh) for salvation. How is this promise being fulfilled and how does it connect with the salvation offered in the *name of Jesus*?

7. Read Acts 2:37-47. How do those listening respond to the message? What are the distinctive practices, habits, and attitudes of this first community of Jesus' followers? Do you see your own congregation represented in this passage? Does your church regularly engage in any of these practices, habits, and attitudes?

Applying God's Word

1. Do you have a Christian friend whose ethnicity is different than yours? How does the story of Pentecost help you to embrace your friend and value them as part of God's multi-ethnic kingdom?

2. Read Acts 1:8. What does it mean to you to be a "witness" for Christ?

3. Read Acts 2:41-47. Which of the practices, habits, or attitudes displayed by the early church in this passage is most challenging for you personally? Where do you need to grow in living out this picture of a Spirit-empowered biblical community in your church and in your daily life?

4. How does the infilling and empowerment of believers by the Holy Spirit radically change our attitude and obedience to God? What new desires has the Holy Spirit given you? What gifts has he given you to use for the building up of others?

Review Timeline and Map

❑ Review the PENTECOST section on the timeline. Note the connection between the cloud icon in the PENTECOST section of the New Testament Timeline and the cloud icon found throughout the Old Testament Timeline.

❑ Review the fifth New Testament Map: *The Expanding Witness of Pentecost*. Find the cities and regions listed in Acts 2:9-11 on the map.

Dig Deeper with the Study Guide

❑ Read the first section of chapter four: PENTECOST, Part 1 (pp.129-140).

The Holy Spirit Empowers Mission

Just as the Father sent the Son into the world, so Jesus sends his disciples into the world. The empowering presence of the Holy Spirit inspires Christian mission into all the earth. There is no people group, no ethnic community, no social or economic status that stands outside the loving reach of our Savior Jesus Christ. The storyline of Acts reveals how Christian witness moves out in an ever-expanding witness. The Holy Spirit gives believers a spiritual burden for those nearby to know Christ, even stirring in them a desire to be reconciled with those formerly ignored or despised. The Holy Spirit creates a profound concern for those who have never had the opportunity to hear about Jesus Christ. The "final days" have arrived and salvation in the name of Jesus is proclaimed to all.

We see this expanding movement of the Holy Spirit reflected in the book of Acts. Jesus extends his kingdom through his disciples empowered by the Spirit, beginning in Jerusalem (Acts 1–7). Christian mission then reaches Judea and Samaria (Acts 8–12), and finally, it expands across great cultural divisions to the ends of the earth (Acts 13–28). Jesus empowers believers, who have received new life in him, and each member of his body has a role to play. Some are called to pray, others to preach. Some are led to serve, others to send. Some are to give their financial resources, while others are to give their own lives for the gospel. In every circumstance and with every life, the gospel of Christ moves out into a world of need.

Early Christian mission grows through preaching, healings, and compassionate care for widows and the poor. Thousands believe in Jerusalem and beyond. Jesus uses suffering in his followers to deepen their commitment and refine their dedication to him. Christian suffering bears witness to our suffering Messiah. He uses cultural opposition to strengthen their resolve and authenticate their witness. Faithful ministry always requires sacrifice. Pruning yields even greater fruit. Peter and John are arrested and yet enabled to bear witness to Jesus among the highest officials in Jerusalem. Stephen, the first martyr, proclaims Jesus as Messiah and is stoned for blasphemy. Yet, his death, like the death of Jesus, causes the kingdom of God to grow and encourages the witness of others. Jesus sends his disciples into Samaria and reconciles traditional enemies to become brothers and sisters in Christ. He reaches into Africa to convert an Ethiopian high official of the court. He calls a Roman soldier named Cornelius, who brings his entire family to hear about Jesus from Peter, a fisherman from Galilee.

Jesus not only reconciles traditional enemies, but he alone has the power to transform the most violent opponent into a dedicated servant. Jesus appears in glory on the road to Damascus and converts Paul from a zealous persecutor of the church into an apostle to the nations. No one is beyond the gracious, redeeming, and transforming embrace of Christ. Self-righteousness is renounced and Christ's righteousness received. Cultural pride is overwhelmed with a love for the church. Jesus calls Paul to make his name known among the nations. The unity of the body comprised of people from different ethnicities and backgrounds heals a fractured world as the global mission of the church extends toward all peoples and nations. All who repent and believe find forgiveness through the cross of Christ. Their shared identity calls forth a new name from the surrounding society, as the disciples are first called *Christianoi* ("Christ-ians") by a wondering world.

As the growing church gathers for worship in Antioch, the Holy Spirit speaks: "Set apart for me Barnabas and Saul for the work to which I have called them" (Acts 13:2). Their work will extend the gospel to the nations and establish local churches who teach believers to follow Jesus in all of life. The narrative of Acts describes this work through an expanding series of missionary journeys that include extended periods of local church planting and discipleship. I encourage you to retrace these journeys on the map together with your own sincere prayer: "What is the work the Holy Spirit is calling me to do?"

Paul's first missionary journey sets sail from Antioch and arrives on the island of Cyprus, Barnabas' home. The ministry team proclaims Christ in the synagogues at Salamis and continues across the island to Paphos, where the Holy Spirit opens the eyes of Sergius Paulus, the Roman governor, to believe in Christ. This is a wonderful beginning of all that Christ will accomplish through those who have dedicated themselves to his service. Paul, Barnabas, and Mark sail north toward the coast of Asia Minor. As they approach the shore, the towering peaks of the Taurus Mountains rise before them. The vast interior province of Galatia lay on the distant horizon, utterly unreached. The Holy Spirit stirs Paul to cross the mountains and reach Pisidian Antioch after ten days. We hear Paul's preaching for the first time in Acts 13:16-41. His sermon proclaims that God's plan of redemption through history has now reached a decisive point in Jesus the Messiah.

Many of the key ideas of our entire CASKET EMPTY study can be found here. Their missionary journey continues east to the cities of Iconium, Lystra, and Derbe, where many Israelites, God-fearers, and diverse nations believe in Jesus Christ. They return to Antioch with the joyous report that the Lord had opened the door of faith to include the nations.

Bible Readings:
**Acts 4:1-12; 7:54–8:4; 8:25-40; 9:1-31;
10:34-48; 13:1-3, 4-52; 15:1-35**

Questions for Reflection

1. Read Acts 4:1-12. How does the persecution of Jesus-followers by Jewish leaders result in an opportunity to share the story of Jesus' resurrection and good news?

2. Read Acts 7:54–8:4. After Stephen preaches his sermon, he is stoned to death by those who reject his message (notice also the presence of Saul). How does God use suffering to accomplish his missional purpose? How is the gospel message expanding?

3. Read Acts 9:1-31. How does Paul (also known by his Hebrew name Saul) go from being a persecutor of the church to a proclaimer of the gospel? What are the key moments in Paul's conversion, and who played important roles in his transformation?

4. Read Acts 10:34-48. Why is this such an important story in the expansion of the gospel to all nations? How do these events relate to what happened at Pentecost?

5. Read Acts 13:1-3. This is the first instance of the church intentionally and strategically sending out missionaries to share the gospel with the world. What steps did the church at Antioch take to select them and then send them out?

6. Read Acts 13:4-52. Notice that Paul in his sermon is rehearsing key events and passages from the Old Testament to demonstrate that Jesus is the Messiah and that salvation is in him alone. How do people respond to the word of God? What events happen in this story that propel Paul and Barnabas to proclaim the gospel to the Gentiles (a term for "nations")?

7. Read Acts 15:1-35. What were the central issues being addressed by leaders of the church at Antioch? How are people from the nations being incorporated into the church? Where does each group practice self-denial to strengthen the body of Christ?

Applying God's Word

1. Read Acts 4:1-12. Although the resistance or persecution that you may face in your lifetime might be less than the more public, severe, and hostile form of persecution that Peter and John face, it can still be an effective context for sharing the gospel. How can you be a witness for Christ by what you say and do in the company of people who are resistant or even hostile to the gospel? List a few specific ways that Holy Spirit may be leading you to be more open about your faith and a more faithful witness to the gospel of our Lord Jesus Christ.

2. Have you ever experienced a time when you have faced persecution for your faith? How has it reinforced what you believe? Has it strengthened your faith and trust in the Lord?

3. How did your ethnic group first hear the gospel, meet followers of Jesus, and be impacted by Christian faith? If you came to faith through your family, how did past generations of your family first hear the gospel and become believers? How does your own story impact how you think about missions and evangelism?

4. Let's consider the story of Paul in Acts 9:10-19 and the part Ananias played in his transformation. What were Ananias' feelings and actions? Did Ananias have any special gifts or position? What words describe Ananias' obedience, courage, actions, and speech to Paul? Now take a moment to pray and ask God to send someone, like Paul, to you that you might pray for them.

5. When you think about missions, do you feel called to go or send? To preach or to pray? To give of your resources or to give your life? Take some time to intentionally pray about this in your prayer time this week. How is God calling you to live your life with a missional focus?

Review Timeline and Map

❑ Review the PENTECOST section on the timeline.

❑ Review the fifth New Testament Map: *The Expanding Witness of Pentecost*. Note the ripple effect that the proclamation of the gospel has as it expands from Jerusalem into Judea and Samaria. You can almost visually see the evangelistic shock waves that impact the region following Pentecost.

Dig Deeper with the Study Guide

❑ Read the second section of chapter four: PENTECOST, Part 1 (pp. 141-162).

The Good News of Jesus Is Shared with All the Earth

THE GOOD NEWS OF JESUS' life, death, and resurrection must be shared with all the earth. Our sacred responsibility recalls the original calling of humanity and anticipates the prophetic vision that "the earth will be filled with the knowledge of the glory of the Lord as the waters cover the sea" (Hab. 2:14). The expansion of the church across geographical and ethnic boundaries continues in Paul's second missionary journey, as the gospel is proclaimed in Europe. After strengthening the newly established churches, the Holy Spirit directs Paul and his companions to Troas, near ancient Troy. During the night, Paul receives a vision of a man from Macedonia urging him: "Come over to Macedonia and help us" (Acts 16:9). All who are without Christ are in desperate need of the good news of Jesus. Luke records that "immediately we sought to go on into Macedonia, concluding that God had called us to preach the gospel to them" (Acts 16:10). Luke now joins the missionary team ("*we* sought to go") and relates what follows from the perspective of an eyewitness. They cross into Europe and proceed to Philippi. The Lord opens the hearts of several people, including a wealthy merchant named Lydia, a young girl enslaved by a spirit of divination, and a Roman jailer who had violently opposed the missionaries. This is the remarkable beginning of the church in Europe.

The missionary team continues west across northern Greece and arrives in Thessalonica, where many believe in Christ, including Jews, God-fearing Greeks, and prominent women. After a brief visit to Berea, Paul is taken to Athens, the intellectual center of the ancient world. He reasons in the marketplace with philosophers and merchants, and in the synagogue with sages and scholars. Finally, he is brought to the Areopagus ("Mars Hill") to defend his teaching. Here on a rocky outcrop with the Parthenon rising directly behind him, Paul proclaims the God whom the Athenians do not yet know. He is the Creator of the world and of all humanity. He is Lord of heaven and earth. He does not dwell in temples made by human hands. From one man, he made every nation and determined their place and time in order that all might seek after him. He now calls all people everywhere to repent from idolatry and to believe in Christ, whom God raised from the dead. The Lord graciously opens the hearts of several people, including a member of the Areopagus Council named Dionysius, a woman named Damaris, and several others who believe. Paul continues south to Corinth, an unreached city with a reputation for commerce, decadence, and immorality. For Paul, it was a long way from home, the farthest place he had yet traveled. It must have seemed overwhelming, but the Lord strengthens him by supplying Priscilla and Aquila as co-workers and soon opens the heart of the synagogue ruler to believe. Paul remains in Corinth for eighteen months and a great number of Greeks, Romans, and Jews believe in Christ and begin to walk in his way together. After visiting the church in Jerusalem, Paul returns to Antioch and encourages the church with all that Christ is doing among the nations.

Paul's third missionary journey sets out again from Antioch to strengthen the churches and to open a new work in the strategic city of Ephesus. Paul remains there for three years to establish a gospel movement that radiates out through others to reach the entire region. Despite intense cultural opposition and persecution, vast numbers of people from diverse nations turn from idolatry and believe in Christ. They renounce magical arts and fall in love with God's word. They reject civic pride and embrace the glory of Christ's everlasting kingdom. Jesus reveals his righteousness in the life of the local church, a holy community of forgiven sinners. After three years in Ephesus, Paul visits the churches in Philippi and Macedonia. He finally arrives in Corinth where he spends three critical months preparing to extend the gospel of Christ to the "end of the earth." He purposes to visit Rome in hope of receiving support to extend the gospel to the western edge of the Mediterranean Sea, the province of *Hispania,* which we know today as Spain. He will need their prayers, gifts, and partnership. He will also need them to understand his presentation of the gospel and vision of the church, that Jews and Gentiles are justified by faith and united to one another in Christ. He introduces himself and his ministry with his longest letter, which we know today as Romans.

Paul's final missionary journey in Acts brings him first to Jerusalem. Despite his warm reception by the Jerusalem church leadership, Paul is arrested in the temple on the false accusation of defiling the sanctuary with foreigners. He is taken into custody and kept under house arrest for two years in Caesarea, where he is able to share Christ before kings and governors. He eventually appeals his case to Nero Caesar and completes a perilous journey in chains to Rome. He first seeks an audience with the Jewish community of the city and announces that "it is because of the hope of Israel that I am wearing this chain" (Acts 28:20). From morning till evening, Paul reasons with them from Scripture and seeks to persuade them about Jesus. Some believe, while others refuse. He then turns his attention to the nations. The narrative of Acts brings us to a hopeful end as Paul stays in Rome for two years, welcoming "all who came to him, proclaiming the kingdom of God and teaching about the Lord Jesus Christ with all boldness and without hindrance" (Acts 28:30-31).

Bible Readings:
Isaiah 2:1-4; Acts 16:14-21; 17:16-34; 20:17-27; 26:1-23; 28:23-30

Questions for Reflection

1. Read Acts 16:14-21. This story records the first converts in Europe. What are the different ways people are coming to faith in Jesus? How does this remind us that the gospel is open to all who would believe?

2. Read Acts 17:16-34. Paul's strategy in Athens is a model for how the gospel can be communicated to people who have spiritual longings, even though they may not yet know about Jesus. Trace each aspect of Paul's communication:

- What does the abundance of idols tell you about the Athenians' spiritual longings (v. 16)?

- How does Paul connect with his audience without judging them (vv. 22-23)?

- How does Paul use Greek poets to bolster his presentation (vv. 27-29)?

- How does Paul call for a faith commitment from his audience (vv. 30-31)?

- What is the response of those who hear (vv. 32-34)?

3. Read Acts 20:17-27. Paul summarizes his life and ministry to the elders of the church at Ephesus. How do his words remind you of the sacrificial life of Jesus? How might his devotion to the Lord encourage you to serve the Lord wholeheartedly?

4. Read Acts 26:1-23. As you read through Paul's testimony before Agrippa and Bernice, what has been the focus of his life after his encounter with Jesus? Describe in a few sentences what it means to be a follower of Jesus based on Paul's own life.

5. As you reflect upon Paul's conversion, compare his life *before* meeting Jesus, and his life *after* his encounter with Jesus. How is this a powerful testimony of a changed life? What stands out to you? How might this encourage you as you share the gospel with others?

6. Read Acts 28:23-30. The book of Acts concludes with Paul as a prisoner in Rome. What are the central aspects of his teaching, even while he is in chains (vv. 23, 31)? How might this shape your priorities?

Applying God's Word

1. Having read Paul's message at Mars Hill, now think of your own neighborhood. What things do you see that reveal the spiritual longings of your neighbors? How could you connect with your neighbors without making them feel judged? What personal story could you tell that could prompt them to open their hearts as you share the gospel?

2. People become open to hearing and responding to the gospel when they are told a personal story, like Paul does in Acts 26:1-23. Take time now to write out four elements of *your* story:

   a. *Before I became a Christian,* I used to think...act ... long for ... (choose one or more)

   b. *But then something happened* (describe a crisis you experienced, a challenge/problem you faced, a new perspective about Christ that changed your mind...)

   c. *And I placed my faith in Jesus* (describe how/when you did this)

   d. *Since becoming a Christian, here is one thing that has changed in me...*

3. Read Isaiah 2:1-4. Allow the prophetic scene of all nations coming to know the Lord to fill your heart with praise. Write out a prayer below. Thank God for your own salvation. Pray for those close to your heart who do not yet trust in Jesus. Invite the Lord to use you as his witness in the world.

Review Timeline and Map

❑ Review the PENTECOST section on the timeline. Note specifically the sections related to Paul's missionary journeys.

❑ Review the sixth New Testament map: *Paul's Missionary Journeys.* Trace the routes of Paul's three missionary journeys as well as his journey to Rome. Take note of the cities mentioned where Paul and his companions establish churches.

Dig Deeper with the Study Guide

❑ Read chapter five: PENTECOST, Part 2 (pp. 163-197).

New Communities Find New Life in Christ

As CHRISTIANS SHARE THE GOSPEL with others, believers gather together in new church communities. The New Testament letters provide teaching to these communities on what Christians believe and how they are to live as followers of Jesus. Twenty-one of the twenty-seven books of the New Testament are letters written by early Christian leaders, such as James, Paul, Peter, and John. These letters are sometimes called epistles, which is simply the Greek word meaning "letter." We will look at seven letters in each of the next three lessons. This week we focus on the important theme that new communities find new life in Christ.

The earliest New Testament letter was written by James, the earthly brother of Jesus. James came to believe in Jesus after his resurrection and became a leader of the church in Jerusalem. His letter is filled with allusions to Jesus' Sermon on the Mount. James urges believers to be "doers of the word, and not hearers only" (Jas. 1:22). New life in Christ is observed in care for the vulnerable, widows and orphans, and in avoiding friendship with the world. We show the character of God in how we live and love one another.

We now turn to consider Paul's earliest letters. On Paul's *first* missionary journey he writes *one* letter. In Galatians, he highlights the power of the gospel to create new life. Paul writes that "I have been crucified with Christ. It is no longer I who live, but Christ who lives in me. And the life I now live in the flesh I live by faith in the Son of God, who loved me and gave himself for me" (Gal. 2:20). Believers are justified by faith in Christ. They are adopted into God's family and filled with the Spirit. The fruit of the Spirit produces new life in all who believe. God's new creation has indeed begun.

On Paul's *second* missionary journey he writes *two* letters. 1-2 Thessalonians describe new life in Christ as faith, love, and hope. Faith in Jesus grants forgiveness; love is faith in action; and hope anticipates Christ's glorious return. Paul recalls how believers turned from idols to serve the living and true God. Believers live a new life and are exhorted to "walk in a manner worthy of God, who calls you into his own kingdom and glory" (1 Thess. 2:12).

On Paul's *third* missionary journey he writes *three* letters (1-2 Corinthians and Romans). 1-2 Corinthians address the pressing questions of new life in Christ asked by the church in Corinth. How does faith in Christ inform marriage and sexuality? Where does new life in Christ cause me to participate in my culture and where do I reject or transform it? What is the meaning of the Lord's Supper? How are spiritual gifts used to build up the body of Christ? What will happen when Christ returns? How should I spend my money? Paul provides wise counsel for growing Christians in that "whatever you do, do all to the glory of God" (1 Cor. 10:31). Romans is Paul's longest letter and his most detailed exposition of how the gospel creates new life in Christ. The gospel reveals God's righteousness by faith to all who believe. All people have sinned and need God's forgiveness. God has provided his own beloved Son as an atoning sacrifice for the sin of the world.

In Christ, he has condemned sin and justifies freely all who have faith in Jesus. Believers are filled with the Spirit and begin to walk in newness of life. The Spirit empowers us to walk in God's ways. We each offer our body as a living sacrifice, holy and pleasing to God. We are no longer conformed to this world but transformed by the renewal of our minds. We recognize and pursue God's will in our lives together. New life in Christ is seen and shared as we join together in support of God's mission to bring the gospel to all the earth.

In this portion of the Bible study, you will be reading selected sections from seven New Testament letters. The letters are presented according to the storyline of the New Testament and not in their canonical order. We encourage you to read each letter studied this week in its entirety. You would also benefit greatly from reading the *New Testament Study Guide*, where you will find more information about authorship, date, historical context, and key topics covered in each letter. Keep the *New Testament Timeline* nearby so that you can identify where each letter is located in the storyline of Acts under PENTECOST and the geographical location of its recipients under TEACHING.

Bible Readings:
**James 1:19-27; Galatians 2:20 and 5:13-26; 1 Thessalonians
1:1-7; 2 Corinthians 3:1-18 and 5:14-17; Romans 5:12-21; 7:4-6;
8:1-13 and 12:1-2**

Questions for Reflection

1. Read James 1:19-27. James encourages believers to be doers
   of the word and to receive the word implanted in them. What
   does it mean to be a "doer" of the word and how do our actions
   signify our new life in Christ? What are some of the qualities
   that ought to characterize Christians?

2. Read Galatians 2:20 and 5:13-26. How is new life in the believer
   being formed? Summarize how Paul describes the "deeds of
   the flesh" in comparison to the "fruit of the Spirit." What role
   does the Spirit have in bringing about godly fruit and what role
   does the believer have in walking by the Spirit? What might
   this mean in your life?

3. Read 1 Thessalonians 1:1-7. What positive effects does the Holy Spirit create in us when we believe the gospel? What else is involved in spiritual growth?

4. Read 2 Corinthians 3:1-18 and 5:14-17. How do these verses describe the new creation work going on inside of you as you trust in Jesus and read and apply God's word?

5. Read Romans 5:12-21. What is the new life offered to believers in Christ and how does it contrast with the old life in Adam? How are we "made righteous"?

Applying God's Word

1. Read James 1:22-27. *Information* (Bible knowledge) is good, but *transformation* (thinking and acting more like Jesus) is the ultimate purpose of reading, studying, and applying God's word. Write down one application step you will personally take in response to verses 26-27:

   a. Bridle/control my tongue/speech:

   b. Visit a vulnerable or afflicted person:

   c. Purity in my thought-life and habits:

2. Read Romans 7:4-6 and 8:1-13. How would you describe your old life that was conformed to the values and attitudes of this world? How does this contrast with your new life in Christ? How might you set your mind on the Spirit? What practical steps might you take?

3. Read Romans 12:1-2. When you sacrifice something for a higher purpose, you are showing serious intent to make that purpose a priority in your life. How can your life choices as a follower of Jesus be a "living sacrifice"? How does such a commitment to Jesus transform and renew our minds so that we can understand and live out God's will in the world?

Review Timeline and Map
- ❏ Review the TEACHING section on the timeline. Note the key New Testament teachings box and the icon explanations relevant to this section on the back of the timeline.
- ❏ Review New Testament Map 6. Locate the cities where these seven letters are sent.

Dig Deeper with the Study Guide
- ❏ Read chapter six: TEACHING, Part 1 (pp. 199-234).

New Communities Are United in Christ

HUMAN HISTORY, CONTEMPORARY SOCIETY, AND our own experience remind us that we live in a broken world. Anger, resentment, and divisions abound in our families, relationships, and among ethnic groups. Hatred, exploitation, and ethnic violence shatter hearts and defile the land. But the gospel reveals another way. God's redemptive purpose at the cross was to reconcile us to himself and to one another. He is creating one new humanity in place of our divisions. He has destroyed our hostility at the cross. He has proclaimed peace to those near and those far. He has joined us together in one Spirit with the same access to the Father. He has declared that there are no strangers, no foreigners, only fellow citizens, fellow members of God's family. He has created new communities who are united in Christ.

In our study last week, we looked at the first seven New Testament letters. This week we are covering the next seven letters, focusing on the profound reality that newly formed Christian communities are united in Christ. Paul now takes his *fourth* journey, this time to Rome. While under house arrest, he writes *four* letters (Ephesians, Philippians, Colossians, and Philemon). These letters all make explicit reference to Paul's imprisonment and are called the Prison Epistles.

Ephesians emphasizes God's plan to unite all things in Christ (Eph. 1:10). The mystery once hidden in God's purpose but now revealed is that the nations of the world are "fellow heirs, members of the same body, and partakers of the promise in Christ Jesus through the gospel" (Eph. 3:6). The church displays God's wisdom to the entire cosmos when we gather in the unity of the Spirit and in the bond of peace. We proclaim that "there is one body and one Spirit … one Lord, one faith, one baptism, one God and Father of all, who is over all" (Eph. 4:4-6). Jesus' atoning death on the cross has torn down the dividing wall of hostility and united us in Christ.

Philippians exudes joy as Paul celebrates an enduring partnership in the gospel. He urges the church to live out her heavenly citizenship in a manner that transforms our divided, earthly society. Above all, he desires to know that the church is "standing firm in one spirit, with one mind striving side by side for the faith of the gospel" (Phil. 1:27).

Colossians is written to encourage the church planted by Epaphras, a man who had come to faith through Paul's extended ministry in Ephesus. Colossians 1:15-20 offers us one of the most beautiful descriptions of Jesus in the New Testament. He is the image of the invisible God. He is the head of the body, the church. He is firstborn from the dead and preeminent over all. In him, all the fullness of God was pleased to dwell. Jesus Christ alone is able "to reconcile to himself all things, whether on earth or in heaven, making peace by the blood of his cross" (Col. 1:20).

Philemon is a short but profound letter. Paul writes to reconcile two men, one a wealthy landowner (Philemon) and one a fugitive slave (Onesimus), both of whom he had led to faith in Christ. Paul urges Philemon to receive Onesimus no longer as a slave but "as a beloved brother" (Phlm. 1:16). This is the reality of God's renewed humanity in Christ. We stand as equal members of God's family, brothers and sisters united in Christ.

Near the end of his life Paul writes three final letters to the next generation of Christian pastors, known as the Pastoral Epistles (1-2 Timothy and Titus). These letters reveal Paul's earnest desire to support future leaders of the church who will strengthen the unity of the church by their teaching. God's mission will be carried out in every generation, including our own. Paul emphasizes the importance of godly character for leadership and the priority of teaching God's word for faithful ministry: "All Scripture is breathed out by God and profitable for teaching, for reproof, for correction, and for training in righteousness" (2 Tim. 3:16). He exhorts Timothy to fan into flame his teaching gift and not to be afraid. He urges Titus to dedicated service and to teach "sound doctrine" (Titus 2:1). Humble Christian service, based on the word of God, points others to Jesus and will create new communities who are united in Christ. What we share as fellow believers in Christ will triumph over anything that threatens to divide us. Ask the Lord where he is calling you to serve today.

Bible Readings:
**Ephesians 1:3-14; 2:11-22; Philippians 2:1-18;
Colossians 1:3-23; and 2 Timothy 3:14–4:8**

Questions for Reflection

1. Read Ephesians 1:3-14. How many "in Christ," "in him," or "before him" phrases can you find in these verses? What does this tell you about what unites us as Christians? What actions are centered in Christ? What stands out to you in this passage?

2. Read Ephesians 2:11-22. God's law connected Jews to God as his covenant people, but tremendous hostility grew between Jews (who took pride in God's law) and Gentiles (who were ignorant of it or distained it). How does this text describe God's perfect solution to bring hostile, fractious people groups into peace with one another and with God? How does this passage contribute to Paul's "in Christ" teaching that we have already seen?

3. Read Philippians 2:1-18. Do you notice that Paul's first (vv. 1-4) and last (vv. 12-16) exhortations to live rightly have the example of Jesus *right at the center* (vv. 5-11)? What are the powerful action words in verses 5-11 that describe Jesus' example that we should follow? How will this lead us into greater unity with other believers?

4. Read Colossians 1:3-23. How do the startling truths declared in this text expand your understanding of the supremacy of Jesus Christ and your appreciation for him (see especially vv. 13-23)? What has Jesus done to accomplish reconciliation? Ask yourself: Where can I be an instrument of reconciliation in my family, my community, or among my people?

5. Read 2 Timothy 3:14–4:8. What are the attributes of Scripture? What positive effect does Scripture have on our lives as we read it and study it? How might Paul's exhortation in this passage encourage you in your reading and studying of God's word? Are there any steps you need to take to pursue more time in the word?

Applying God's Word

1. Having read Colossians 1:3-23, take ten minutes to pause and praise God in prayer for each one of these qualities and actions of Jesus, then meditate in prayer on Jesus' exalted place in the universe. Paul says later in the chapter that the mystery is that Christ "is in you, the hope of glory." Meditate on the wonder of the exalted Christ dwelling in you—the hope of glory. Write a short reflection on what this means to you.

2. To increase your application of God's word in your life, write these application questions in your Bible or in a notebook and use them whenever you read Scripture. Using Colossians 3:1-25, answer the following questions:

What truth is here that I can rejoice in?

What example can I imitate?

What error should I avoid?

What promise of God is here that I can trust?

What mystery is here that I can ponder and ask God to reveal it?

3. What Bible study habits could you cultivate this week?

4. How can you strengthen the unity of the body of Christ where you may be tempted to cause division?

Review Timeline and Map
  ❑ Review the TEACHING section on the timeline.
  ❑ Review New Testament Map 6: *Paul's Missionary Journeys.* Locate the cities that Paul wrote to that were discussed in this week's text.

Dig Deeper with the Study Guide
  ❑ Read chapter seven: TEACHING, Part 2 (pp. 235-262).

New Communities Are Faithful to Christ in Suffering

CHRISTIANS TESTIFY TO JESUS' DEATH and resurrection as the center of God's plan of redemption. We proclaim forgiveness of sins for all who believe in his name. All nations are invited into God's family as co-heirs with Christ. These glorious truths confront human pride, challenge societal norms, and are often opposed. Christians are maligned and misunderstood. They suffer personal injury, estrangement from family and friends, and loss of property. Sometimes believers bear witness to Christ even unto death. In every circumstance, we follow the example of Jesus who prayed for those who crucified him and did not retaliate when he was attacked. He remained faithful in suffering, and he requires that his followers do the same.

In our study this week, we are looking at the final seven letters in the New Testament, focusing on how new communities are faithful to Christ in suffering. The Scriptures teach us that suffering matures our faith, opens the gospel to others, and presents an irrefutable testimony that Jesus is alive. These last seven letters are written by four different authors: Peter, the writer to the Hebrews, Jude, and John. Each of these letters teaches us how to respond, how to endure, and how to remain faithful in difficult times.

Peter writes two letters to encourage Christians who are suffering (1-2 Peter). He reminds believers that "Christ also suffered for you, leaving you an example, so that you might follow in his steps" (1 Pet. 2:21). He urges Christians to pray for those who persecute them and writes: "If anyone suffers as a Christian, let him not be ashamed, but let him glorify God in that name" (1 Pet. 4:16). Even though our adversary the devil prowls like a roaring lion, believers are exhorted to remain faithful to Christ. We know that the same kinds of sufferings are experienced by Christians throughout the world. When one part of Christ's body suffers, we all go to our knees in prayer.

Hebrews is unique among the New Testament letters. Although its author and location are uncertain, what is absolutely certain is that the author holds a breathtaking view of Jesus Christ. He describes the Christian life with rich vocabulary and makes extensive use of the Old Testament. His words of exhortation encourage believers to remain faithful to Christ above all, even when facing persecution, imprisonment, and the plundering of their property. He exhorts us not to neglect meeting together out of fear but "run with endurance the race that is set before us, looking to Jesus, the founder and perfecter of our faith, who for the joy that was set before him endured the cross, despising the shame, and is seated at the right hand of the throne of God" (Heb. 12:1-2).

Jude is a short letter written by one of Jesus' earthly brothers. Jude calls the church "to contend for the faith that was once for all delivered to the saints" (Jude 1:3). Christians must guard against false teachers who turn the grace of God into a license for sin. God saved us by grace that we might live in holiness before him. God's judgment will be revealed against those who claim Christ as Savior and yet deny him as Lord. We remain faithful to Christ, knowing that he will keep us from falling and present us blameless before his glorious presence with great joy.

The final three letters of the New Testament are written by the apostle John (1-3 John). He knows of no greater joy than to hear that Christians are walking in the truth and abiding in the teaching of Jesus. He warns believers to test the spirits since many false prophets have gone out into the world: "Every spirit that confesses that Jesus Christ has come in the flesh is from God, and every spirit that does not confess Jesus is not from God" (1 John 4:2-3). As we remain faithful to Christ, even in the midst of suffering, our faith in Jesus Christ grows deeper. We are able to share the love of our suffering Savior with others who are suffering. We will also share the victory of his resurrection and enjoy eternal life with him forever.

Bible Readings:
1 Peter 1:3-9; 2:21-25; Hebrews 11:1–12:3; 13:20-22;
Jude 1:24-25 and 1 John 4:1-6

Questions for Reflection

1. Read 1 Peter 1:3-9. What is the source of believers' hope and joy amidst suffering? List how we are to respond during times of suffering and trials. How has God been at work in your own life during similar seasons?

2. Read 1 Peter 2:21-25. Reflect upon Jesus' example in verse 23. Why is this so hard to do? How does God use this response to persecution to change the fallen human pattern of endless revenge and retaliation?

3. Read Hebrews 11:1-40. How do these examples of "people of faith" encourage us in our faith today? How is suffering woven into their lives and how did they persevere in the faith?

4. Hebrews 12:1-3 speaks directly to persecuted and suffering Christians in the first century (and to us today). Like a grandstand of spectators cheering on the foot-racing competitors, who are the "great cloud of witnesses" who encourage us to run the race set before us? Like racers who build endurance through physical training and personal coaching, how can Christians build spiritual endurance? Who do we keep our eyes upon, and why him?

5. Read 1 John 4:1-6. The Greek word for "test" means to examine for genuineness. What does John say is the test that reveals whether a prophet, preacher, or teacher is truly from God? Why do you think this is so important?

Applying God's Word

1. Read Hebrews 12:1-3. Paul's charge to "run with endurance the race that is set before us" suggests movement, looking forward, and making progress. What is the next *action step* in your "race" through hardship, opposition, or suffering because of your faith in Jesus?

2. Read 1 Peter 2:21-25. Reflect upon one follower of Jesus who has demonstrated dignity and Christ-like character while suffering because of his or her faith in Jesus (this person could be from the past or living presently). What character traits do you admire in them, and how did God use suffering redemptively in their life to bring positive change?

3. Read Hebrews 13:20-22 and Jude 1:24-25. Read aloud these "benedictions" and insert your own name whenever "you" is mentioned (i.e. "Now to him who is able to keep [your name] from falling…"). Let this good, life-giving encouragement fill your mind, calm your heart, and make your soul confident in God, who, through Jesus, came to the lowest places of suffering himself, so that you might stand before the presence of God. What is one aspect of these benedictions that is meaningful to you?

Review Timeline and Map

❏ Review the TEACHING section on the timeline.
❏ Review New Testament Map 6: *Paul's Missionary Journeys* again.

Dig Deeper with the Study Guide

❏ Read the first section of chapter eight: TEACHING, Part 3 (pp. 263-280).

Seven Key Beliefs Define Christianity

THE NAME "CHRISTIAN" WAS FIRST given to believers by the surrounding community (Acts 11:26). This name was not based on their ethnic identity, class, or social standing but on their *unity* in Christ—they were called *Christ*-ians. What did others observe that caused them to call them Christians? What beliefs do followers of Jesus hold in common? How do these beliefs shape the way that we live? How would you answer the question: "What do Christians actually believe?"

In our study this week, we will learn about seven key beliefs that unite Christian teaching, define Christian identity, and motivate Christian witness. These beliefs fill the New Testament letters and are central to the life and vitality of the church throughout the ages. These truths define Christianity. Learning them will help us remain faithful to the Lord and guard what he has entrusted to us.

The first key belief is that *Jesus is the Messiah, Christ the Lord*. Jesus is the fulfillment of God's redemptive promises in the Old Testament. Jesus is the promised Son of David and the reigning Son of God who rules over God's everlasting kingdom. The New Testament letters emphasize that Jesus Christ is Lord. To call Jesus

"Lord" affirms his divinity, authority, and glory. As Messiah and Lord, Jesus draws all people to himself and invites them to receive everlasting life through belief in his name.

The second key belief is *justification by faith*. The patriarch Abraham believed in God, and by God's grace, he was justified by faith. All who believe in Christ are declared righteous by faith in Christ alone. The atoning death of Christ provides forgiveness for the sin of the world. God's righteous wrath against sin is fully satisfied at the cross. We are saved by grace, God's unmerited favor, revealed to us in the face of Jesus Christ. Faith in Christ identifies God's new covenant people.

The third key belief is *the presence of the Holy Spirit*. God had promised through the prophet Joel that the Holy Spirit would be poured out on all flesh. The Holy Spirit confirms our adoption into God's family and empowers our new life in Christ. The Holy Spirit teaches us to pray, provides joy in the midst of suffering, and inspires our worship. The gifts of the Holy Spirit are used to build up the body of Christ and to bear witness to Jesus in the world.

The fourth key belief is that *Jews and Gentiles are "one in Christ."* God had promised that all nations would be blessed in Abraham's descendant. The New Testament teaches that in Christ the Gentiles (the nations of the world) are "fellow heirs, members of the same body, and partakers of the promise in Christ Jesus through the gospel" (Eph. 3:6). Both Jew and Gentile find forgiveness through Christ's death. Both find new life in Christ's resurrection. We are one people, reconciled to God and to each another. This truth is not found anywhere other than in Christ.

The fifth key belief is *obedience of faith among the nations*. In the Old Testament the prophet Ezekiel had seen that obedience would come through the indwelling Holy Spirit. Obedience is an essential aim of the Christian life. Our joyful obedience to Christ by the power of the Spirit brings pleasure and praise to God the Father.

Through Jesus Christ "we have received grace and apostleship to bring about the obedience of faith for the sake of his name among all the nations" (Rom. 1:5-6). Transformed lives offer compelling public evidence that Jesus died and is alive today.

The sixth key belief is that Christians are called to be *living sacrifices, "holy to the LORD."* God had set apart Israel as his holy people, and believers now fulfill this holy calling as God's own possession. Holiness means being "set apart unto God" for his purpose in the world. We are not our own but belong to God. We live as a kingdom of priests, mediating between God and people. We bear the suffering of others and intercede in earnest prayer, knowing that forgiveness and healing are found in Christ. The Lord is our portion, and we seek to reflect his glory in every aspect of our lives.

The seventh key belief is that *Christ will return in glory as Judge.* Jesus is the exalted Son of Man, who is given dominion, glory, and a kingdom. Christians call all people to repent and turn to Christ in faith, knowing that all will appear "before the judgment seat of Christ" (2 Cor. 5:10). In view of Jesus' second coming, Christian mission is carried out with great urgency. Christ's visible return in glory is God's victorious ending. Evil will be condemned. The dead will be raised to everlasting life. The righteous will be clothed with immortality. God will dwell with his people in a new heavens and earth forever.

We should devote our primary teaching and disciple-making energy to these key beliefs. We sometimes take major truths for granted and give our attention to secondary topics in the body of Christ. Differences among committed believers in secondary areas should never obscure the radiant light of these key New Testament beliefs that create, sustain, and distinguish Christian community.

Bible Readings:
**Romans 1:1-6; 2:8; 5:1-11; 15:15-19; 2 Corinthians 5:9-11;
Ephesians 2:19-22; 3:1-12; 1 Peter 2:4-10; and Revelation 20:12**

Questions for Reflection

1. Read Romans 1:1-6. *Jesus is the Messiah, Christ the Lord.* Why does
   Paul start his letter this way and what does it tell you about
   the centrality of Jesus? How is Jesus seen as Lord in Paul's
   life—and in *your* life?

2. Read Romans 5:1-11. *Justification by faith in Christ.* Like the front
   doorway is the entryway into an entire house, "justification"
   in verse 1 is the doorway into all the blessings listed in the
   verses that follow. Make a list of the blessings in this passage
   and thank God in prayer for each one.

3. Read Ephesians 2:19-22. *Indwelling presence of the Holy Spirit.* What terms are used to describe the church in these verses? Notice that believers are being built *together* into a dwelling of God in the Spirit. What implications does this have for your relationship with fellow believers?

4. Read Ephesians 3:1-12. *Jews and Gentiles are "one in Christ."* How is the life, death, and resurrection of Jesus (who lived 2,000 years ago in a country and culture very different from yours) relevant and redemptive to you? What does Paul say in this passage that leads you to believe Jesus does impact how you see yourself and others? How does Paul persuade us that Jew and Gentile are "one in Christ"?

5. Read Romans 15:15-19. *Obedience of faith among the nations.* How does Paul define his mission and how is it being accomplished? How does the work of the "Spirit of holiness" connect to obedience in the life of the believer?

6. Read 1 Peter 2:4-10. *Living sacrifices, "holy to the Lord."* Peter's description of New Testament believers recalls God's calling of Israel to be a holy people, which he now applies to the church (see Exod. 19:5-6). Write out a description for each of these attributes that Peter declares is true about people who are followers of Jesus:

   • Chosen race

   • Royal priesthood

   • A people of God's possession

- Called out of darkness into God's marvelous light

- God's people

- Recipients of mercy

7. Read 2 Corinthians 5:9-11 and Revelation 20:12. *Christ will return in glory as Judge.* People everywhere cry out for justice to be served, for wrongs to be made right, for crippling debt to be removed, and for evil to be punished. Christians believe that *longing for justice* is evidence that our Creator is a God of justice. How do these passages stir in us an urgency to preach the gospel, which is motivated by God's coming judgment of all people?

Applying God's Word

1. Read Romans 5:1-11. How do these verses show the depth of God's love for you? Say a prayer of thankfulness to God for his love.

2. Now that you've studied these seven central beliefs of the Christian faith, which one stands out to you and why? How has the Holy Spirit been stirring your heart through God's word this week?

3. How might you grow in your knowledge of central Christian beliefs so that you are able to stand firm in the faith? What steps do you need to take?

Review Timeline and Map

❑ Review the TEACHING section on the timeline and review again the Key New Testament Beliefs section.

❑ Review New Testament Map 6: *Paul's Missionary Journeys*

Dig Deeper with the Study Guide

❑ Read the final section of chapter eight: TEACHING, Part 3 (pp. 281-294).

Jesus Rules the World and Gathers His Church

THE FINAL BOOK OF THE Bible is a "revelation of Jesus Christ" (Rev. 1:1). Revelation is not primarily a book about the "end times" but about Jesus Christ. Revelation means "to unveil." We are allowed to see the Lord as he rules the world and gathers his church. The vision of Jesus in Revelation replaces fear with faith, compromise with conviction, and complacency with courage. God is in control and his purposes will prevail. The book of Revelation should be read as a single, extended vision of Jesus. He is exalted Son of Man and Lord of the church (Rev. 1–3). He is worshiped in heaven and is worthy to carry out God's eternal purpose on earth (Rev. 4–5). He releases a measured wrath and gathers an innumerable multitude from all nations (Rev. 6–11). He triumphs over Satan's counterfeit kingdom and extends his own kingdom without end (Rev. 12–15). Jesus will one day return in visible glory and final victory (Rev. 16–20). He will condemn evil forever and create a new heavens and earth where righteousness dwells (Rev. 21–22). When we see Jesus, our hearts are encouraged. Our resolve grows stronger. Dedication to his kingdom becomes our highest priority. Faithful witness to his salvation becomes our greatest joy.

Like Israel's prophets in the Old Testament, Revelation reveals God's perspective on our present circumstances and his promises for the future. Jesus speaks to his people as Lord of the covenant and holds the nations accountable as Lord of all the earth. In Revelation 1–3, Jesus addresses seven churches in a series of letters to cities in Asia Minor. These are real congregations facing temptations of compromise with the world, lukewarm spiritual life, false teaching, and societal persecution. These are the same temptations that the church faces today. Each letter begins as Jesus speaks with divine authority and admonishes his people to remain faithful. Each letter ends with a warning for those who would betray him and a promise of blessing for those who remain loyal to his cause. In Revelation 21–22, Jesus shares the promised blessings with all who believe and share his victory. The book of Revelation inspires hope for the future and motivates faithful following today.

We see the breathtaking scope of Christ's redemption in the heavenly scene of worship. Jesus is the Lamb of God, slain before the foundation of the world. With his atoning blood he has ransomed people for God from every tribe, language, people, and nation (Rev. 5:9). They are welcomed into his everlasting kingdom and will reign with him upon the earth. Jesus gathers his church through the faithful, often suffering, witness of his people. His power is made perfect in weakness. His gospel is heard through humble, human voices. We see the results of our testimony in the innumerable multitude from every nation, from all tribes and peoples and languages, crying out with a loud voice, "Salvation belongs to our God who sits on the throne, and to the Lamb!" (Rev. 7:10).

When reading Revelation, keep your attention on Jesus Christ. You see him as he is right now. Grow confident in his power, authority, and saving activity in the world. Receive his loving rebuke and anticipate his promised reward. Allow the Holy Spirit to purify your imagination with the radiance of God's splendor. Turn your affections away from all counterfeit powers. Renew your commitment to Christ in light of his glorious appearing. Trust his sovereignty and grace, even when the world seems to have the upper hand. Overcome by the blood of the Lamb and by the word of your testimony. Refuse all worldly weapons or ambitions. Follow the Lamb wherever he goes. Pray that he might use your life, your family, and your church to help gather in the harvest of the nations.

Bible Readings:
Daniel 7:13-15;
Revelation 1:1-18; 2:1–3:22; 5:9-10 and 7:9-17

Questions for Reflection

1. Read Revelation 1:1-18. This visionary description of Jesus is vivid and awe-inspiring. What do these images tell you about Jesus and his authority now? What stands out most to you?

2. Read Daniel 7:13. You may recall that we studied Daniel's prophecy in the period of EXPECTATIONS, noting the importance of the heavenly vision of the Son of Man ruling over God's everlasting kingdom. Why does John cite this passage and what is he describing (Rev. 1:6-7)? How might this vision encourage those who are suffering? How might this vision inspire the complacent? How might this vision motivate Christian witness in the world today?

3. Read Revelation 2:1–3:22 (select *one* church from this section):

   • What does Jesus *know* about this church?

   • What does Jesus *recognize* is good in this church?

   • What *rebuke* does Jesus give to them?

- What does Jesus *tell them to do?*

- What *promise* does Jesus give them?

4. Read Revelation 5:9-10. Jesus, the sinless Son of God, died for our sins. His blood paid a ransom that frees us from sin-caused separation from God. To whom is this ransom available? How might you respond in worship?

5. Read Revelation 7:9-17. You may recall that John the Baptist was the first to recognize Jesus as "the Lamb of God, who takes away the sin of the world" (John 1:29). Now we are given a glimpse of the exalted Lamb of God who receives praise and honor from the great multitude gathered before him. What elements of this heavenly scene are most beautiful and poignant to you? Why?

6. What Old or New Testament themes do you notice in these verses? How do they reinforce that the Bible is one redemptive story with *Jesus at the center*? Notice *who* is at the center of this scene of heavenly worship, which is a foretaste of all eternity.

Applying God's Word

1. Read Revelation 1:12-13. "I saw seven golden lampstands, and in the midst of the lampstands, one like a son of man." Imagine the lamps burning with oil upon their stands in this vision and the light they shine into the darkness. How is your church shining the life and light of the gospel of our Lord Jesus into the darkness of *your* community?

2. Imagine your church is being spoken to like one of the seven churches of Revelation 2 and 3.

   • What does Jesus *know* about your church?

   • What does Jesus *recognize* is good in your church?

   • What *rebuke* would Jesus give to the members of your church?

- What does Jesus *tell* you to do?

- What *promise* does Jesus give you?

Review Timeline and Map

- ❑ Review the YET-TO-COME section on the timeline.
- ❑ Review New Testament Map 7: *The Spread of Christian Witness.* Note how the gospel spreads to new regions during the first two centuries.

Dig Deeper with the Study Guide

- ❑ Read chapter nine: YET-TO-COME Part 1 (pp. 295-320).

The Glorious Return of the King

GOD'S REDEMPTIVE PLAN THROUGH HISTORY is brought to climactic conclusion in the glorious return of King Jesus and the coming new creation. Jesus' return brings righteous judgment on evil and gracious salvation for all who put their trust in him. His final victory over evil will cause our hearts to rejoice. We will praise him for his justice and celebrate our redemption. The joyous ending of God's saving purpose is compared to a wedding feast, the messianic banquet. We are invited to sit at his table for the marriage banquet of his beloved Son. He will clothe us with fine linen, bright, and pure. We will see his face and live with him forever. Jesus Christ rides forth in final victory. He is "Faithful and True" (Rev. 19:11). He is crowned with authority and bears the divine name. His robe is dipped in redeeming blood. The armies of heaven follow him in triumph for he is "King of kings and Lord of lords" (Rev. 19:16). The outcome of the final battle is never in doubt. God's people stand and see the salvation of the Lord. Jesus defeats the beast, the false prophet, and the dragon, the ancient serpent who opposed God's kingdom from the beginning. The tyranny of evil is condemned. The Son of Man is vindicated. Jesus sits enthroned as powerful Savior and heavenly Judge. All humanity who have ever lived appear before him. Death and those who share the culture of death are banished. His everlasting kingdom is conferred on all who love and trust him. They will live and reign with him forever in righteousness. Hallelujah! Worthy is the Lamb of God!

After God's victory over evil, sin, and death, God creates "a new heaven and a new earth" (Rev. 21:1). Israel's prophets longed for the day when God would recreate the heavens and the earth where righteousness dwells. Evil and sin would be banished. Death and violence would be no more. The new heavens and earth would endure as the sanctuary of worship for all of the redeemed. Resurrected life will be shared by fellow citizens of God's eternal city, the New Jerusalem, which is the centerpiece of the new heavens and earth. The New Jerusalem comes down out of heaven adorned as a bride for her husband. The Lord will wipe away every tear from our eyes, and death shall be no more. There will no longer be mourning, crying, or pain, for the former things have passed away. The Lord promises: "Behold, I am making all things new" (Rev. 21:5). The city of God is holy, resplendent with the glory of God. The city is secure with a high wall, strong foundations, and twelve gates. The city is massive in size with ample room for the innumerable multitude from every tribe and nation who walk by its light. The city is built with precious stones and jewels that recall the Garden of Eden, but now fellowship with God has been restored. God and humanity are reconciled. As his image-bearers, humans fill the earth with God's glory and enjoy the work of their hands.

When we look inside the New Jerusalem, we see "the river of the water of life, bright as crystal, flowing from the throne of God and of the Lamb" (Rev. 22:1). The river flows out from God's dwelling through the city to renew the earth. Beside the clear, life-giving waters, the tree of life grows alongside the banks of the river. The tree bears twelve kinds of fruit, one for each month. The leaves of the tree bring healing to the nations. In the opening chapters of the Bible, access to the tree of life in the Garden of Eden had been lost. Fellowship between God and humanity had been shattered through the deception of sin. Redeemed humanity now regains access to the tree of life at last. No longer will there be any curse. God's people will live under his blessing. They will walk in newness of life. They will reflect his image in loving and wise care of the earth. They will fulfill their original mandate in the beauty of holiness and glorify him forever.

The revelation of Jesus Christ ends with eager anticipation as Jesus promises his bride: "Behold, I am coming soon" (Rev. 22:7, 12). God's people live in hopeful expectation of Christ's return. Jesus calls us to faithful witness and dedicated service until the day of his appearing. He will reward all who love and trust him. He is "the Alpha and the Omega, the first and the last, the beginning and the end" (Rev. 22:13). Revelation closes the biblical canon with a warning. If anyone adds to Scripture, God will add to him the plagues described in this book. If anyone takes away from Scripture, God will take away his share in the tree of life and in the holy city, which are described in this book. The canon of Scripture is complete from Genesis to Revelation. God has written all that we need for life and salvation. There are no new revelations. There are no other books. There are no additional prophets to draw our attention away from Jesus Christ, the Lamb of God, who was slain for us. He declares with everlasting authority: "Surely I am coming soon." His expectant bride answers in reply: "Amen. Come, Lord Jesus!" (Rev. 22:20).

Bible Readings:
Genesis 3; Revelation 19:1-9; 20:11-15; 21:1-27 and 22:1-21

Questions for Reflection

1. Read Revelation 19:1-9. What are the elements of a wedding banquet, feast, or reception in your own culture? What customs are practiced? During the wedding *ceremony* most people are *watching*, but at the wedding *banquet* everyone *participates*. How is the wedding banquet in Revelation a wonderful image describing the celebration in heaven that all believers in Jesus will share?

2. Read Revelation 20:11-15. God's final judgment is depicted in this vision. How might this stir in us thankfulness for our salvation and an urgency in making Jesus known?

3. Read Revelation 21:1-9. What aspects of heaven described here are most impactful to you? Which blessing do *you* most long to experience personally?

4. Read Revelation 21:10-27. The New Jerusalem is a breathtaking picture of God's new creation. How might this vision encourage you to persevere in your faith and to live your life with a purpose, knowing what lies ahead?

5. Read Genesis 3 and then read Revelation 22:1-5. How does this picture of heaven show how our human story has come to a beautiful and redemptive completion because of Jesus? Remember that the tree of the knowledge of good and evil had tempted Adam and Eve to sin in the garden. How does this picture of a restored Eden complete God's plan of redemption?

6. What is the difference in how Adam and Eve responded to God's presence after the Fall (see Gen. 3:7-10), in comparison to how we will experience and respond to God's presence in heaven?

7. Read Revelation 22:6-21. These are the final verses of the Bible. What stirs your heart in this passage and how might the Lord want you to respond?

Applying God's Word

1. Revelation is much more than a "happily ever after" ending to our human story. Take a few minutes to ponder Revelation as a vivid and redemptive completion to our human story. Write out (and tell God) a short prayer of thanks for what Revelation describes will be our experience in heaven.

2. Jesus taught us to pray, "Your kingdom come, your will be done, on earth as it is in heaven." What aspect of God's heavenly kingdom described in Revelation are *you* praying will be done on earth in your lifetime? What is your next step to act accordingly with that prayer?

3. Revelation describes beautiful and awesome acts of worship offered to God by people (redeemed by Christ), angels, and all creation. What do you notice is being said and done? What sounds (and silences) happen? Who is the focus of worship? After responding to these questions, take moment to ponder your church's worship services, which are "glimpses of heavenly worship." What might *you* do to prepare for your church's worship service that reflects the heavenly worship as described in Revelation?

4. Now that we have reached the end of our study together, write a few reflections on what you have learned in this study and what the Holy Spirit has been stirring in your heart. If you are doing this study in a small group or Sunday school, take the time to share with one another how God has been speaking to you through this study and pray for one another.

Review Timeline and Map
    ❑ Review the YET-TO-COME section on the timeline.
    ❑ Review New Testament Map 7: *The Spread of Christian Witness.*

Dig Deeper with the Study Guide
    ❑ Read chapter ten: YET-TO-COME Part 2 (pp. 321-345).

Invitation of Response

As we conclude our study, it is eternally important to remember that God's redemptive plan addresses each one of us today. God invites us to become part of his story through faith in Jesus Christ. If you have never put your faith in Christ for salvation, we would like to personally invite you to do this now. You can use the following prayer as a guide:

Almighty God, I have come to see the greatness of your person and your plan. I confess my own sinfulness before you and humbly repent of all of the ways in which I have dishonored or disobeyed you. I put my faith right now in Jesus Christ. I believe that you have placed my sin upon him. The righteous wrath that I deserve, you have poured out upon him at the cross. His righteousness is now my own. Christ's empty tomb is death's defeat. His resurrection is now my hope. Fill me now with the presence of the Holy Spirit. Teach me to walk in newness of life. Use my life in any way you choose to extend your mission in the world. Keep my eyes fixed on you, Jesus, my promised Messiah and coming King. I will worship you with all my heart both now and forever. In Jesus' Name, Amen.

If you have prayed this prayer, we encourage you to share this with your pastor or small group leader, as they can pray for you and help you on your journey with Jesus. If you already know Jesus Christ and this material has strengthened your discipleship, or if you are using this material in a mission context, we would love to hear from you. You can send an email through the Casket Empty website (casketempty.com).

May the Lord bless each of you as you live and announce the good news of Jesus Christ in the power of the Holy Spirit. May he capture your heart and mind as you continue to study and delight in his inspired Word. May he use the Church as his instrument to reflect the radiant glory of God's renewed humanity in Christ. May he call each of us to join God's mission in the world today as the gospel of the kingdom continues to extend to all nations. Amen.

David Palmer and John Moser

Guidelines for Leaders

WE ARE DELIGHTED THAT YOU have embarked on this CASKET EMPTY Bible Study. It is a privilege and great blessing to lead God's people in a journey through the New Testament so that together we might grow deeper in our love for God and in our knowledge of his redemptive plan revealed in the Scriptures. Since this study covers the entire New Testament, it can feel rather intimidating to lead this kind of study, especially for a lay leader. It takes years of study to feel confident teaching the entire New Testament, but you do not need to be an expert. Others are not expecting you to have all the answers. You are embarking on a journey *with others,* as you study God's word *together.* There are some practical steps you can take ahead of time to prepare for the weekly studies so that you are an effective small group leader.

Getting Started

This Bible study has been designed as a weekly small group study or Bible class. As you get started, it is important to give a few weeks lead time so that people can order a copy of the Bible study and the companion *New Testament CASKET EMPTY Timeline* and *Maps.* Having the material in-hand ahead of time gives people time to become familiar with the Casket Empty acronym and how it works. Videos on the Casket Empty YouTube channel can be useful for those who are unfamiliar with the biblical narrative. Having a few weeks of lead time also gives you an opportunity to invite new people to the study who might not already be part of a small group. The Casket Empty website has Bible study invitation cards available that can be downloaded free of charge. You simply need to add your church information and the dates for your study, and then have the cards printed at your church or through a local printer. If you are doing this study in a larger church setting with a companion preaching series, you may want to consider having a promotional Casket Empty (vertical) banner printed and displayed in your church. The artwork for the promotional banner is available on the Casket Empty website as a free downloadable file that can be emailed directly to a local printer. The promotional files are designed for your church use so that you can advertise your Bible study, whether by personal invitation or on your church website. Videos on how to teach Casket Empty in your local church setting (available on our Casket Empty YouTube channel) will enable you to hear directly from Pastor John Moser as you prepare your church for this journey. Lastly, if you are doing this study as part of a larger group, your church may want to consider purchasing the large timeline wall banner (15ft in length), which can be displayed in the room where your study will be held. Information about promotional materials and the large banner is available on the Casket Empty website (casketempty.com).

Weekly Preparation

Each week participants will be reading several chapters of the New Testament and answering questions related to its content and application. You will need to set aside time each week to do the Bible readings and discussion questions. Spend time prayerfully reading the Bible passages, and if you need to read additional chapters so that you are familiar with the content, it is well worth the effort. Ask God to give insight into his word, and prayerfully consider how it applies to your life, using the application questions as a guide. In addition to completing the readings and questions, one of the best ways you can prepare to lead your Bible study is to read the companion *CASKET EMPTY New Testament Study Guide.* At the end of each weekly Bible study, page numbers from the Study Guide are given that correspond to the Bible study. You will gain an in-depth understanding of the New Testament by reading the relevant sections of the Study Guide ahead of time, and it will build confidence in you as a leader. The Study Guide should be your first "go to" resource, as it can function as a leader's guide for this study. Another resource you will find helpful is a Study Bible (such as the ESV or NIV). This will give you further insight into specific verses so that you can be prepared for questions that may arise in your small group. Lastly, when preparing for your Bible study, it is vital that you locate the biblical passages within the larger storyline of the New Testament. This is especially important for the New Testament letters, as you want people to connect them to the storyline of Acts. The best way to do this is to keep the New Testament timeline in front of you. Always, always review the redemptive storyline so that you have a clear sense of what you have studied so far, and where you are headed. The *Casket Empty New Testament Maps* are also a vital aspect of the learning process, as they trace visually the ministry of Jesus and the missionary expansion of the church. As a leader, it will be vital that you help your group see the "big picture" of the storyline and keep them on track as they journey through the New Testament. People will need encouragement each week since the New Testament Bible study is longer than most six or eight-week studies. It is your job as the study leader to help people see where they are headed so they do not feel overwhelmed or get lost in the details. If this Bible study is part of a church-wide curriculum with a corresponding preaching series, weekly sermons will reinforce what you are study-ing in your group and help to integrate small groups into the life of the church.

Schedule

This New Testament Bible study is designed to be done over the course of fourteen weeks. When used with the companion *CASKET EMPTY Old Testament Bible Study*, it provides a thirty-two-week study through the entire Bible. Since the New Testament is fourteen weeks, you may decide to do the study in two seven-week segments, with a week or two weeks break in between (and a longer break during Advent). This allows people to process the content over time. The study can also be done consecutively, potentially begin-ning in the fall (with a break over Advent), and then continuing into the new year. Alternatively, you could start the Bible Study in January, and study the Bible over the course of the year (with a break over the summer). Ideally, you should set aside eighty to ninety minutes for the weekly group meeting. If you are doing this study on Sunday morning before or after church (and you only have one hour), you'll need to decide which questions to discuss together as a group, and you'll need to be careful with time management.

Leading the Study

There are several ways to lead this Bible study, and it will depend on what format is most suitable for your church context. If you are doing this study in a small group, eight to ten people are ideal, meeting at church or in someone's home. Once the group has gathered and you have welcomed people, there are a few options for the first ten to fifteen minutes. One option is to begin each week by inviting feedback from the group about what they have learned during the week, or you could ask them to highlight one thing that has been meaningful to them. There is high flexibility in the type of introductory questions. The goal is for people to interact with each other before you dive into the study questions. The advantage of this approach is that you will learn quickly about the felt needs of your group, and you may want to shape the discussion as a result. The second format requires you to take a more active teaching role by providing some introductory comments. The advantage of this approach is that it gives you an opportunity to review the lesson, and you can remind the group where they are headed. Depending on your level of comfort, this can provide an opportunity for questions even before you break into groups. If your church has purchased the large New Testament wall banner and it is on display, you can give your introductory remarks *in front* of the banner. This enables you to walk people through the New Testament visually, and you can point to key areas on the timeline that are relevant for the weekly study. This approach has the advantage of reinforcing what is being studied by providing a strong visual component, something that is central to the Casket Empty curriculum. If you are doing this study as part of a larger Bible class, this format works particularly well. Once you have done your introduction, the larger group can then break into smaller discussion groups, with each group having its own leader. Depending on the time frame for your weekly study, you may need to decide ahead of time which questions you will discuss as a group since you may not have time to discuss all them. Make sure you leave time for the application questions, as this ensures that people have an opportunity to share about how God's word applies to their lives. Lastly, it is important to conclude your weekly study with a time of prayer. This forms a bond with your group, and it fosters community as your group learns to care for one another and concerns are brought before the Lord. As you step out in faith as a Bible study leader, may the Lord equip you to teach his word, and may you do so in confidence, knowing that God's word will not return empty without accomplishing what he desires. May the study of God's word always lead you to the living center who is Jesus Christ our Lord.